Contents

John B. Anderson,
U.S. Congressman, Illinois:

"A well-informed and highly readable look at one of the world's great civilizations, a remarkable nation suddenly and mysteriously opening up before our very eyes. Stan Mooneyham's explication is an illuminating one that I have very much enjoyed reading.

His observations on the church in China provide both fresh insights and new hope."

Father John P. Bradley, M.A. (Oxon.)
Provost Belmont Abbey College
Belmont, North Carolina:

"A first-rate book providing the reader with invaluable insight into the history and culture of China, insights which provide the key to a proper understanding of the recent Great Leap Outward. However, for western Christians, the book's most important message is the lesson which the uninstitutionalized Christian church in China, purified in persecution, can teach us."

Russell Chandler,
religion writer, *Los Angeles Times*:

". . . Easy to read, well-documented, and presents a compelling case that Mao's socialist humanism was actually used by God to set the stage in this new day for a mighty wave of biblical Christianity to sweep over the giant empire of the 'Middle Kingdom.' "

Dr. Richard C. Halverson,
Fourth Presbyterian Church,
Washington, D.C.:

"A well-written, insightful introduction to China—past, present, and future, in depth and in hope. Timely and relevant for the church and mission."

CHINA:

A NEW DAY

CHINA:

A NEW DAY

by

W. Stanley Mooneyham

Logos International
Plainfield, New Jersey

CHINA: A NEW DAY
Copyright © 1979 by W. Stanley Mooneyham
All rights reserved
Printed in the United States of America
Library of Congress Catalog Card Number: 79-83789
International Standard Book Number: 0-88270-364-1
Logos International, Plainfield, New Jersey 07060

To my grandson,
Blake,
with whom
China will have to share
the twenty-first century

Prologue

The Long March was over.

When the big man with the rough peasant hands stood on the red brick "Gate of Heavenly Peace," he faced south just as countless emperors before him had done.

Mao Tse-tung savored the moment as he proclaimed the People's Republic of China with the word, "Today the Chinese people stand erect!" His Communist followers had achieved in four years what had evaded the Japanese Imperial Army in fourteen years—the conquest of all China.

The date was October 1, 1949.

The ex-farmer boy from Hunan had just launched the bloodiest reign in China's 3,000 years of written history. During that reign he managed to accumulate a record of sorts. According to *Guinness Book of World Records*, Mao Tse-tung was responsible for the deaths of more people than any other person who ever lived.

In 1976 Mao himself died and went to his just reward. Waiting in the wings to take leadership of the country was another participant in the Long March. A pragmatic, tough little walnut, at just under five feet tall, he didn't cut the figure of a Mao Tse-tung, but he had proved his staying power through numerous purges. In character and speech he was as pungent as the spicy food from his native province of Szechwan. Soon elevated to the post of deputy premier, Teng Hsiao-p'ing began to set the nation of nearly one billion people on a different course for what he called "The New Long March."

He released political prisoners, rehabilitated disgraced intellectuals and promised restoration of rights and property to capitalists. He also established diplomatic relations with Mao's No. 1 enemy, the United States of America.

Much of the world is holding its breath to see if the feisty little politician can keep the ancient land on the course he has set. If he does, you and I may be living in the exciting early dawn of China's new day.

1
The Great Leap Outward

China? There lies a sleeping giant. Let him sleep, for when he awakes he will move the world.

Napoleon Bonaparte

The giant empire which has for centuries slept in a reclusive torpor of self-satisfaction is now awake—and Napoleon's prophetic statement suddenly takes on new meaning.

China has already begun to move the world, and statesmen, economists and scientists are dusting off another prophecy, this one by historian Arnold Toynbee who said, "The twenty-first century will belong to China. They will be two-fifths of the human race by then."

The momentous events of recent months have caused me to recall an isolated incident in my own life which took place in Communist East Germany nearly fifteen years ago. Some friends and I were leisurely window-shopping one evening in the city of Leipzig. Two Russian army officers, recognizing that we were not Germans, came up for some conversation.

On discovering that we were Americans, their excitement intensified.

"Russia and America must be friends," they insisted. We assured them we, too, wanted friendship, but that we didn't think Russia was acting all that friendly in those days.

They brushed aside the barb and continued the friendship pitch: "Our countries must be friends so that when the time comes we can join together to fight our common enemy."

Knowing full well what they meant, nonetheless we pretended we didn't and asked if they were talking about Germany. They glanced over their shoulders as their voices grew hushed: "Nyet, nyet. The big country in the East—China."

Even then the Russians were shaking as they contemplated the prospect of an awakened China spreading her influence over the earth. It was a fear shared by much of the rest of the world. The threat of the "yellow peril" is a recurring theme throughout history. Russia's fears may be rooted in the bear's proximity to the dragon—after all, the two countries share a common border which stretches 4,150 miles, the longest land boundary in the world.

For most of the rest of the world, however, it was a fear based on ignorance.

Our Mutual Misunderstanding

In fact, it was what we didn't know that made China seem so fearsome. To us, both the land and its people were mysterious. We talked about the "inscrutable Chinese" and chafed at the smugness revealed in a facial expression that seemed never to change.

America's preoccupation with Europe because of our ancestry is probably responsible for our long indifference to China. If we thought about it at all, it was the world of the "heathen Chinee" where everything was upside down, where dogs were eaten and children were sold into slavery, where women bound their feet and men smoked opium and played mah-jongg.

Our misunderstanding had been fed by a longstanding prejudice which also was based on ignorance. Horace Greeley may have been euphoric about America's far west, but he had a decided antipathy for the Far East. Writing in the *New York Tribune*, this nineteenth-century journalist characterized the Chinese as "uncivilized, unclean and filthy beyond all conception . . . lustful and sensual in their disposition; every female is a prostitute of the basest order."

Even though we progressed beyond that libelous stereotype, we still knew so little of the truth that we classed all Chinese in one of two Hollywood images.

There was the wise and soft-spoken Charlie Chan who always had a Confucius saying on his tongue and bemused tolerance for his bumbling "Number one son." Then there was the wily and sinister Fu Manchu who could cut your throat with one look through those narrow slits that were his eyes and who was always planning evil.

We were never sure which one was the real China, but we assumed that one of them had to be. We were in general agreement with Will Rogers—we liked the ones we had met. The unfailing courtesy and graciousness of the man who did our laundry always impressed us and we watched with some envy the pleasant togetherness of the family which cooked and served our corn soup and chop suey.

But somewhere, we mused, there must be the Fu Manchus hiding in the rice paddies and it was that unknown element that aggravated our fears. That China might one day be the common enemy of Russia and America was not unthinkable in the mid-1960s.

The idea probably wasn't ruled out in Peking either, for misunderstanding was a two-way street. The Chinese have never been well informed about the rest of the world. It hardly seemed necessary when you thought of your country as the world's center. Couple this introspective mentality with the natural boundaries formed by mountains, deserts and the Pacific Ocean and the result is a totally insular people.

When China's Communist rulers came to power

they turned the nation even more inward and added some prejudices of their own. The controlled press carried only unfavorable stories about the United States. The regime divided the world into two groups. There were the true friends of China and then there were the "running dogs and lackeys of American imperialists."

A generation of Chinese youth grew up on anti-American slogans and the army did its bayonet practice on scowling images of Uncle Sam.

The Big Switch

But things have changed. And if you think your mind is boggled by the 180-degree turn of events, imagine what it must be like for the average Chinese who, having been told that Coca-Cola is a symbol of the complete decadence of the capitalist West, is now going to be able to buy it at his local commune PX!

Picture his consternation as he reads the wall posters in Peking—which once denounced the United States along with its "lackeys and running dogs," but now include words in English like "Love," followed by phrases of friendship toward the former enemy.

On this side of the Pacific, the public is only slightly less amazed as it reads a statement by a leading senator declaring that President Carter's decision to normalize relations with the People's Republic of China "finally brings American policy into line with Asian realities" and learns that China has bought a 1976 Hollywood science fiction epic, *Futureworld*, for screening in theaters all over the country.

And that is only the beginning of astounding announcements. Intercontinental Hotels signed a half-billion-dollar agreement to build and operate a chain of luxury hotels across the country and *Time* magazine named China's Vice Premier Teng Hsiao-p'ing its 1978 "Man of the Year."

The recognition was bestowed, *Time* said, "Because of the tremendous enterprise he has launched to propel the nation into the modern world." In popular parlance the big switch is called the Great Leap Outward, but the Chinese leaders themselves refer to the remarkable change as the New Long March in an obvious effort to establish its legitimacy. The first Long March was a turning point in the Communist revolution as Mao Tse-tung led 100,000 of his followers on a perilous trek from the southern province of Kiangsi to the mountain reaches of Shensi province near the Mongolian border. There they regrouped to carry on the fight against the Nationalists.

The New Long March is toward the twenty-first century and what has become known in Chinese rhetoric as the Four Modernizations—an attempt to update agriculture, industry, science and technology, and defense, all simultaneously.

The Peking *People's Daily* becomes rhapsodic as it

contemplates the goal: "The Chinese people's march toward the great goal of the Four Modernizations echoes from the foothills of the Yenshan Mountains to the shores of the Yellow Sea to all corners of the world and has aroused world-wide attention. We are setting out to conquer on our New Long March the mountains, seas, plains, oil fields and mines of our motherland. We want to scale the heights of science and technology. We want to develop normal trade relations with other countries of the world."

A billboard in Shanghai, showing Chinese youth astride galloping horses, carried the slogan: "Take advantage of every minute, every second, to race to the year 2000."

So China, having moved at a snail's pace for centuries, is now rushing toward the future.

How the Change Came

The revolutionary road over which China now hurtles has, after countless twists and turns, brought them from the caves of North China to plush corporation board rooms in New York. That trek is even more dramatic than the Long March.

It never could have happened while Mao Tse-tung was living. The old warrior was too doctrinaire a Marxist to condone fraternizing with the enemy. Making revolution was more important than making friends. He was the consummate revolutionary when he wrote: "A revolution is not a dinner party, or writing an essay, or painting a picture, or doing embroidery; it cannot be so refined, so leisurely and gentle, so temperate, kind, courteous, restrained and magnanimous. A revolution is an insurrection, an act of violence by which one class overthrows another."

He unleashed the Cultural Revolution in 1965 in order to purify the movement and keep the revolutionary fires burning in the hearts of young people who never had a chance to shoulder a gun for the cause. It was a totally wrenching experience from which the nation still has not recovered.

Under the banner, "Better red than expert," Mao turned China into a vast social experiment. He had no use for specialists, technicians and bureaucrats because he viewed them as the new elite. They were different from "the people" and must learn to "serve the people." So during the Cultural Revolution, offices and laboratories were emptied and thousands of officials, doctors and scientists were stripped of their privileges and sent off to farms and factories to experience a political conversion.

To Chairman Mao, being "red" meant you knew all the socialist theory and championed it with revolutionary fervor while the "expert" was merely functional. If you were expert, you only knew how; if you were red, you knew why.

And red was better.

The movement was also anti-intellectual. Universities were closed and teachers as well as students were dispersed throughout the countryside to "serve the people."

By every criterion which could be applied, the Cultural Revolution was a failure. Not only so, it nearly wrecked the country. Using one unit of measurement, the *People's Daily* charged that leaders were interested only in "political accounts, not economic accounts. As a result, accounting work was greatly weakened and financial management was very confused."

Which is undoubtedly a considerable understatement.

In the early 1970s a start was made to dismantle some of Mao's revolutionary experiments. The process has speeded up since his death two years ago, but the country is still feeling the effects of it. Nearly half of all agricultural specialists in the country are presently working in jobs unrelated to their field. In one province alone, more than one-third of all scientists and technicians are not employed in their specialties.

A survey conducted by the *Kwangming Daily*, which speaks for Chinese intellectuals, found that thousands of highly trained scientists and technicians are underemployed. The paper said it found lab technicians working as sales clerks, radar specialists raising pigs and computer scientists employed in distilleries. The paper concluded that this misuse of the country's best brains has "had serious effects on development" and "remains one of the most pressing problems" facing China today.

The Cultural Revolution did, however, set the stage for the New Long March. The struggle between "red" and "expert" revealed that the two streams of thought—ideological vs. pragmatic—have existed in the Party for a long time. Mao believed that the secret of revolutionary success is not in what a man knows (his expertise), but in how he thinks (his redness).

His premier, Chou En-lai, and others did not share that view. Among the others was the tough and resilient survivor of many Party fights, Teng Hsiao-p'ing. He had been up and down so many times that his career must have looked like a rubber ball. But he had never been out. He was Chou's protégé and may have, in fact, drafted the former premier's last public speech in which he outlined agricultural improvement as one of the Four Modernizations.

When Mao died, Teng—who had been a victim of the zealots during the Cultural Revolution—made another amazing comeback. During his days of disgrace, he had been forced to ride around Peking in a truck with a dunce cap on his head while the Red Guards jeered. His enemies, among whom was Mao's wife, must have thought it was the *coup de grâce* to have him assigned as mess boy in the cafeteria of a Party school.

But they failed to reckon on the "old school" ties which Teng had established throughout the Party hierarchy over the years and on the tenacity of the little man, who is one inch less than five feet tall. As he says, "What storms haven't I braved and what worlds haven't I faced up to?"

He must be savoring his revenge. Now he is Vice Premier and primary architect of the Great Leap Outward. He has lived to see Chiang Ch'ing, Mao's widow and his archenemy whom he blames for the excesses of the Cultural Revolution, arrested as one of the discredited Gang of Four. He has arranged the release of more than 100,000 victims of the Cultural Revolution who were in prison or assigned to forced labor. At the same time, he has presided over the purging of thousands of Red Guards and petty officials.

He has put China firmly on the road toward the twenty-first century. His pragmatic approach to progress seems to signal that the country may become a pinker shade of red.

But whether that happens or not, no one would deny that Teng Hsiao-p'ing is definitely expert.

What Does It All Mean?

The average Westerner tends to read these contemporary events with a rosy optimism, and that is very dangerous. One year does not establish a trend in a country with 5,000 years of history behind it. The knowledgeable China-watcher will even treat ten years with caution.

This is not the first time China has chosen to use the West to accomplish Chinese goals. Even now the word "friendship" is likely to be used in a utilitarian way with little or no emotional content. One of the current slogans of the modernization movement is "Make foreign things serve China." It is not the creative work of a Peking public relations firm. It is an old philosophy which has been brought out and brushed up for the new generation. It was last used 100 years ago when another reformer set about to push the ancient kingdom forward.

He was Feng Kuei-fen who, on observing the difference between China and the rest of the world, was moved to ask: "Why are the Western powers small yet strong, while China is large yet weak?" His answer was: "China has spiritual greatness but the foreigners had the practical know-how." Feng then proceeded to tackle the problem of China's backwardness by sending students abroad, collecting Western scientific literature and building railroads. Sound familiar? China's newest slogan simply updates his nineteenth-century rationale: "Use the instruments of the foreign barbarians without adopting their ways."

His efforts were short-lived, however, as the nation once again began to turn inward just before the dawn of the twentieth century. It is a cycle often repeated in China's history. The changes we are seeing today may mean a great deal. Or, conversely, they may mean nothing at all in the long run. The Great Leap Outward is merely the latest swing of a pendulum which hasn't stopped swinging for centuries.

Time points out a certain familiarity about the current movement by reminding us that ". . . the characters in these recurrent historical dramas seem to bear an uncanny resemblance to one another." Even Mao had his counterpart in China's first emperor, Ch'in Shih Huang, who lived in the third century B.C. Ch'in, too, was impatient with scholarly pursuits and ordered 460 Confucian teachers buried alive. He then ordered a national book burning of all texts which didn't deal with practical subjects like agriculture and fortune telling. So Mao's twentieth-century attack on Confucius wasn't all that original.

This *yang*-ing and *yin*-ing—or moving between two extremes—has developed in the Chinese psyche an ability to cope. It is expressed even in their literature. The most popular historical novel in China, *The Romance of the Three Kingdoms*, opens with these words: "They say that the momentum of history was ever thus: the empire long divided, must unite; long united, must divide."

To the Western mind that is strange talk. We are accustomed to thinking of history as a straight line—a steady flow—with each successive generation building on the progress of the previous one. Success and failure are not thought of as cyclical. Failure, which we regard as abnormal, is meaningful only if the experience keeps us from failing again. To think about swinging between the two extremes throughout a lifetime would drive many of us to quit the human race.

But even nature tends to confirm for the Chinese the cyclical, rather than the linear, movement of history. Periods of peace and prosperity which produced population growth have been followed by periods of famine and disaster which decimated the population.

And so it has been throughout China's 3,000 years of recorded history.

The Changing Face of China

Now comes along a little man with big plans who says he intends to break the cycle. If Mao wanted to change China's heart, Teng Hsiao-p'ing is more concerned with changing its face. He is quite candid about the nation's backwardness: "If you have an ugly face," he muses, "there is no use pretending you are handsome. You cannot hide it, so you might as well admit it."

But the Four Modernizations will require more than cosmetic surgery. If Chou En-lai's dream of turning "a poverty-stricken and backward country into a socialist one with the beginnings of prosperity in only twenty years or more" is to be realized, his protégé will have to make radical changes fast. The flurry of activity on virtually all fronts signals that Teng intends to do just that.

Those intellectuals who were sent out from their laboratories and classrooms to "serve the people" are being brought back and reinstated so that they may serve the New Long March. In Szechwan province alone 12,000 scientists and technicians have been returned to their old jobs. Teng's earthy rationale: "It is better to allow them to work than to have them sitting in a privy, producing nothing."

Amazingly, the United States is being held up as the best example of why this is necessary and proper. In a very favorable article about production in the U.S.A., the *People's Daily* reported: "In the absence of hard work by a large number of workers and scientists, it is impossible to imagine that U.S. production could have reached today's level and impossible to imagine how the U.S. could send men to the moon."

It just so happens that one of China's new scientific goals is to begin launching space laboratories and probes by 1986.

Research in such advanced areas as atomic science, semiconductors, computer technology, lasers and automation has been given priority. This in a country that was smelting pig iron in backyard furnaces only ten years ago.

Between 500 and 700 Chinese will be enrolled in American colleges and universities by September, 1979. By the same time, 3,000 students will be sent to sixteen industrialized, non-Communist nations.

Elite schools have been established and given the best teachers and facilities. Until recently, intellectuals were sneered at as "stinking persons of the ninth category." The other eight categories included "renegades, spies, landlords and bad people."

Teng knows that attention must be given to the sick educational system if the industrial goals of the modernization program are going to be met. With almost five times the population, China's gross national product is only one-fifth that of the United States. Per capita income is less than $400 a year. Automobile production is pegged at one worker, one car, one year. In Japan the ratio is ninety-four cars per worker per year.

The only way the nation can come close to narrowing the huge gap is to import foreign capital and technical aid. For a country that has traditionally been suspicious of all things foreign, that represents quite a leap. Indeed, it is such a radical departure that the *Kwangming Daily* has felt it necessary to put an ideological foundation under the Great Leap Outward. "It is completely un-Marxist," the intellectual journal editorialized recently, "to adopt the foolish attitude of being complacent and arrogant and of uncritically excluding foreign science, technology and culture. We advocate learning from the strong points of all nations."

China is talking about all kinds of big deals with several countries, including the development of her natural resources, but the ones consummated thus far have been relatively modest. One reason is that while the land is potentially rich, it is presently poor and the government simply does not have the cash to pay for what it needs.

Some of those primary needs are in agriculture, which is also one of the Four Modernizations. Much farming is still done by manual labor and it is estimated that China needs one million tractors, 320,000 trucks and at least three million combine harvesters. Just to keep all that equipment repaired and serviced will require 700,000 mechanics and technicians. The government wants to mechanize agriculture by 1980 and be virtually self-sufficient in the production of cereal grains by 1985.

If Teng can achieve even most of his goals, he will have succeeded in substantially changing the face of China in the next twenty years. The cost, according to one rough estimate, would be a staggering $800 billion by 1985.

It is a daring and ambitious undertaking.

It just could be that the little man with the big plans may find it is too ambitious.

What Makes Teng Run?

But that he is trying with might and main cannot be disputed. And no one would accuse him of small thinking and timid planning. In Henry Kissinger's view, "He's a man of no mean consequence."

If the diminutive dynamo appears to be in a hurry, it can safely be said that he is.

There are at least two reasons. First, he is seventy-four years old. He knows that almost certainly he will not be around to herald the arrival of the twenty-first century. Consequently, what he does, he must do quickly.

It would be a major setback for the world if Teng were to die before his programs are solidly in motion. The Bamboo Curtain, having opened ever so slightly, might well be snapped shut again for decades. There would certainly be a massive struggle internally between "red" and "expert." A. Doak Barnett of the Brookings Institute says, "There are still some people in the Politburo who probably don't like the trends."

While the protagonists for each view have struck an accommodation at the highest levels of leadership, the tug of war undoubtedly intensifies with each new decision. Mao's successor as chairman and premier, Hua Kuo-feng, is himself more comfortable with the philosophy of the "great helmsman" than he is with the pragmatism of Teng. On occasion he even sounds like Mao as he preaches the doctrine: "Politics is the commander, the soul of everything, and failure to grasp political and ideological work will not do."

Sinologist Kenneth Leiberthal sums it up this way: "While all current Politburo members desperately want rapid modernization, Teng and his supporters are willing to transform China at a greater cost to the core values of the Chinese Revolution than are Hua and his supporters."

Hua is only fifty-seven—and Teng must be goaded on by that knowledge as he watches the sand run out of his own hourglass.

Second, if the feisty vice premier can get China locked into the orbit of non-Communist nations before his time comes, those who come after him will find it much more difficult to turn the country inward. Ross H. Munro, former resident reporter in Peking for the Toronto *Globe and Mail*, believes that Teng is "setting up booby traps for any neo-quasi-Maoists who might try to renege on the commitment to modernization and try to return China to insularity. When Teng is dead, China will still have commitments to foreign creditors that will force it to continue pushing exports and internal economic development. . . . If current trends continue for a decade, it is hard to conceive of China extricating itself from the orbit even if the modernization drive falters within the country."

Teng is counting on that and he knows he can't afford to lose a second if he is to leave the imprint of his pragmatism on the ancient kingdom before he dies. At this point in his life, time is not his friend.

Before the twenty-first century comes around, China's Great Leap Outward will have become for Teng personally his great leap upward. He acknowledges that. In speaking of his lack of formal education, Teng said, "The kind of university I was in has no graduates. Its name is society. The day I meet God is when I will graduate, and who knows how many grades I will get from God?"

Indeed, who knows?

But this much can be said with some certainty. If China doesn't go back to sleep, from whatever vantage point the man whose name means "Little Peace" views the great century, he will see the nation he stirred from slumber still moving and shaking the world.

2
It's Still the Middle Kingdom

There is nothing new except what is forgotten.

Anonymous

The tourist guidebook to Peking refers to it as the "Temple of Heaven," an impressive building that dates back to the glorious days of earlier empires. It was in this auspicious place that the great emperors gave thanks to their deities for battles won and for seasons of plentiful harvest. It was also the hallowed ground where they held dialogues with the forces of heaven.

As you climb to the uppermost terrace you will immediately notice a most interesting geometric pattern. The ground is laid out in massive stone slabs, arranged in bands around a point in the center. Each single band is made up of nine more stone slabs, decreasing in size toward the center.

In the middle lies a round stone. This stone, the

Chinese will tell you, is the "center of the earth."

This round piece of rock reveals, perhaps as much as anything, the history of China, the beliefs of its people and the mentalities of its leaders. The stone is mute, but the message is clear: "This is where true culture lies—in China. No need to go further for enlightenment. The truth is here."

In Chinese writing, the two characters for the word "China" are *Jung gwo*, literally the "Middle Kingdom." When used in ancient manuscripts, it referred to the civilized part of the world as contrasted with the barbarians who surrounded China. It was not intended to sound arrogant; it was objective fact. There was no ancient civilization comparable to that which had been developed by the Chinese.

Jung gwo has considerable depth of meaning which doesn't come through in the literal translation. It is more than geography, although that is a part of it. In addition to speaking of a place, it also implies a state of mind as well as a philosophy.

The concept has become so deeply embedded into Chinese consciousness that it affects all of life. It is a state of mind which influences every Chinese, no matter where he lives. He belongs to a race of people around whose homeland the universe has supposedly revolved since time began.

If that creates in the Chinese a feeling of superiority, it is not without some justification. The "people of Han"—a designation which comes out of the pre-Christian Han Dynasty—have the longest continuous history of any nation. It spans 5,000 years with 3,000 years of it being recorded. As early as 1500 B.C. the Chinese had developed a sophisticated political system. It organized society and gave to the people property and labor laws, encouraged the arts and sciences, exalted philosophy and regulated commerce.

All this was going on while Europe was still shrouded in the fog of pre-history.

Unlike European culture, however, the Chinese developed mainly in isolation. The inhospitable approaches of desert, mountains, seas and jungle is the primary reason. Located geographically in the heartland of the vast region east of the Hindu Kush Mountains, China is in truth the Middle Kingdom of Asia. It was virtually inaccessible until the fifteenth century. Europe basically left it alone and the very name by which the area is called—the Far East—reflects the early mentality of most Westerners.

This solidly entrenched sense of *place* has given the Chinese a deep-seated personal identity. For all the differences of province, dialect, food and political persuasion, each Chinese has one thing in common. He or she is a member of the "Middle Kingdom." The most ignorant, illiterate Chinese peasant has always known this. Teachers have taught it. Students have believed it. Emperors have proclaimed it.

This single idea of China being at the center has obsessed every Chinese throughout the millennia of their history. It has penetrated into the deepest, most unconscious recesses of the Chinese mind—Nationalist, Marxist and Confucian.

The reason is that "middle-ness" is wholly compatible with the Chinese way of thinking which abhors all excesses of behavior. This has produced a philosophical base called the Doctrine of the Golden Mean. It is the key to understanding Chinese thought and action. In his book, *My Country and My People,* Lin Yu Tang illustrates it this way: "In the West one scientist is infatuated by the idea of heredity and another is obsessed by the notion of environment, and each one goes about doggedly to prove his theory with great learning and stupidity, whereas the Oriental, without much cerebration, would allow something for both. A typically Chinese judgment is: *A* is right, and *B* is not wrong either."

He goes on to say that the use of the term "Middle Kingdom" "is more than a geographical notion. It signifies a way of life which, by holding on to the mean, the normal and the essentially human claims, as the old scholars did, that they have discovered all the essential truths of all schools of philosophy."

How to Manipulate Barbarians

As a result of this attitude, the Chinese people developed a xenophobic contempt for foreign cultures. The country had suffered many times under foreign rule, but the people had never met an equal, much less superior, foreign culture.

To the traditional Confucian scholar, it made no sense whatever that crude ruffians from the frontier should not appreciate China's great superiority. Since the emperor himself had a "mandate from heaven" to rule all men under the sun, he naturally felt it his imperial duty to demonstrate a paternal benevolence to all such "men from afar."

This was not to say that one had to be open and honest with them. Since they were obviously and demonstrably inferior, it was quite acceptable— even necessary—to humor the foreigners with professed sincerity and gifts aplenty. These things in the right balance could win their trust and avoid difficulties later. It was a policy based on meeting China's needs, not befriending foreigners.

However, this friendship approach got an emperor named Ch'i-ying into difficulty—not with the foreigners who rather liked the soft soap, but with conservatives in the emperor's court who viewed such fawning behavior as beneath superior beings. Ch'i-ying found it necessary to defend the policy and drafted a most interesting and revealing defense called *The Memorial of 1844*.

It contains many statements of use in understanding the contemporary situation, so I am quoting from it at some length. I have put the key sentence in italics because I believe it must not be forgotten if we would try to grasp the significance of China's foreign policy actions today.

The methods by which to conciliate the barbarians and get them under control . . . could not but shift about and change their form. Certainly we have to curb them by skillful methods. *There are times when it is possible to have them follow our directions but not let them understand the reasons.* Sometimes we expose everything so that they will not be suspicious, whereupon we can dissipate their rebellious restlessness. Sometimes we have given them receptions and entertainment, after which they have had a feeling of appreciation. And at still other times we have shown trust in them in a broad-minded way and deemed it unnecessary to go deeply into minute discussions with them, whereupon we have been able to get their help in the business at hand.

This is because the barbarians are born and grow up outside the frontiers of China, so that there are many things in the institutional system of the Celestial Dynasty with which they are not fully acquainted. Moreover, they are constantly making arbitrary interpretations of things, and it is difficult to enlighten them by means of reason. . . .

If we should abruptly rebuke them, it would be no way of shattering their stupidity and might give rise to their suspicion and dislike. . . . To fight with them over empty names and get no substantial result would not be so good as to pass over these small matters and achieve our larger scheme.

Sometimes, however, the barbarians from the West chose to operate from their own exalted and superior positions. China has never had the exclusive market on cultural superiority. It must be said, however, that they are more subtle and less blatant about it than the West. It was this battle of wills—with each party assuming it was superior—that led to naked conflict in the past.

China usually lost the battle, but you somehow got the feeling she was winning the war.

Come and Be Changed

And the reason you got that feeling was because of another Chinese principle—this one is called *lai hua*. It means "come and be changed."

The words have an evangelistic ring to them and they can be said with meaning only by someone who has the authority to back them up. China has demonstrated that authority. History shows that the world's encounters with China have changed the world more than they have changed the Middle Kingdom. The massive, amorphous nation seems to possess the remarkable capacity to assimilate and absorb foreign cultural intrusions until they are no longer identifiable as being foreign.

The barbarous Mongols came and stayed for a while. When they were finally beaten and left, they took more of China with them than they left of themselves in China. The alien Manchus had a similar experience with their dynasty. They adopted Confucian ideology and maintained the Chinese institutions which came with the conquered territory. They were defeated; China remained.

As rivers flowing into the ocean lose their separate identities, so China absorbed those diplomatic and trade tributaries which flowed into her from the peripheral Asian countries as well as from Europe and Russia. They either left not to return or they stayed and were changed.

China's attitude toward foreign trade was a projection of its tributary mentality. The self-sufficient and culturally superior Middle Kingdom had no need for things foreign. (Mao would have agreed with that philosophy; Teng would not agree.) Nonetheless, the kind emperor permitted a large variety of trade missions to come to China in order to show favor to the barbarians and as a means of winning their good will. Trade was a privilege to be bestowed by the emperor, however, not a right to be insisted on.

Those who came and asked for the privilege were expected to perform the Chinese ritual of *kowtowing* (literally "knock head," or kneel and touch the ground with the forehead to show submissive respect) before the emperor. There is an interesting story about the emissary of England's King George III, Lord McCartney, who declared such behavior beneath his dignity. It is said that he did finally manage to come down on one knee. If he had performed the full homage, history might tell a different story about British and Chinese relationships.

Emperor Ch'ien Lung sent McCartney away empty-handed except for a letter to the king. It said in part:

Our dynasty's majestic virtue has reached every country under Heaven and kings of all nations have sent their tribute by land and sea. We possess all things; we are not interested in strange and costly objects and we have no use for your country's products. . . .

The request that your merchants may store and trade their goods in Peking is . . . impracticable. My capital is the hub and center around which all the quarters of the earth revolve. Its laws are very strict and no foreigner has ever been allowed to trade there. This request is also refused.

Now it was Britain's turn to be indignant. The

East India Company wanted trade with China and what the East India Company wanted, she usually got.

China Changes at Gunpoint

So for the glory of the British Empire and the gain of the East India Company, gunboats shot their way into China and trade was established—for the first time—on Western terms. It was a shameful chapter in European history as France, Germany and Russia joined England in inflicting indignity after indignity on the beaten land. Opium, which the Chinese rulers had forbidden, was forced upon the people through the ports opened by the "unequal treaties" which resulted from military victories. The conquerors scorned the "weak man of Asia" as each carved away Chinese territory into foreign centers of influence.

In the end, it was China which kowtowed as the land was raped, pillaged, drawn and quartered. In his book, *The Church in China*, William H. Clark calls it, "Humiliation and agony such as China had never experienced in its 4,000 years of recorded history. The despised and feared foreigners, those hairy, high-nosed, seemingly uncivilized barbarians, actually seized much Chinese territory, dominated her economy, threatened her very existence and civilization as nothing had ever done."

The Middle Kingdom lay prostrate.

And the stage was set for the cataclysmic events of

the twentieth century.

The Librarian from Peking

In the early part of that century, there must have been many Chinese who dreamed of the empire's ancient days of glory and longed for their restoration. But it is one thing to dream; it is another thing to do.

From among the many dreamers, one was to emerge as the man with a plan. He was a little-known assistant librarian at Peking University by the name of Mao Tse-tung. Born in 1893 of peasant stock, he early acquired the conviction that China held within it future greatness, a grandeur that would surpass even the accomplishments of the early dynasties.

Everywhere he looked in China he could see only chaos, corruption and weakness. There was no central government worth the name. The country was in the control of rich landlords and brutal warlords. The peasants, caught between, were eternally abused and oppressed.

In the foreign enclaves which had been established in the treaty ports, no one seemed to care what was happening outside. The semi-colonial foreign powers took no responsibility for the collapse of the economy and the resultant social disorder. Inside their protected world was order and insularity. Outside, the country was falling apart.

China was rapidly ripening for revolution.

In July, 1921, inside the French Concession at Shanghai, the Chinese Communist Party was founded by twelve delegates. The representative from Hunan province was the young librarian, Mao Tse-tung. These few kindred spirits believed they could change China and make her once again a nation respected—perhaps even feared.

The ideal of China's restoration burned like a fever in their hearts. For years the revolution was carried to the hills, into the caves, up savage rivers and over treacherous peaks. They fought in the heat and in the snow. No road was too dangerous, no enemy too great.

The self-appointed savior of China was Mao Tse-tung. It was as if he had received his personal "mandate from heaven," like the ancient emperors before him, to exorcise from China the evil foreigners and their capitalistic greed. The man and his thought fused into an image of revolutionary power that promised the ultimate restoration of China's dignity—the embryonic vision that the nation would one day again be regarded as the center of things. In that day, foreigners would come crawling back to an awakened China and then it would be China's turn to accept or reject.

The revolution wore on for twenty-eight years. Mao became its leader. His forces were depleted, but the vision never dimmed.

On October 1, 1949, the old revolutionary stood in front of the masses of Peking to proclaim the beginning of a new era—the People's Republic of China. Every Chinese knew what he meant as his words rang out over Red Square from the Gate of Heavenly Peace: "We have stood up!" On the eve of his victory Mao had declared that China would "never again be an insulted nation."

The library at Peking University was just a short distance away, but the trip had taken nearly thirty years and tens of thousands of miles.

And the former librarian was now the Chairman.

How Marxist, How Chinese?

When the fighting was over, the revolution had just begun. There was a country of 500-600 million people to be made over. Year after year, movement after movement, purge after purge—Mao began to shape a new China.

But a strange contradiction developed. The terminology was new but the sentiments were straight out of the Middle Kingdom. Harvard historian John King Fairbank pointed out that "the more he seeks to make China new, the more he seems to fall back on old Chinese ways of doing it." The Red Guards, for example, strongly resembled the Boxer bands of peasant youth who were commissioned to eliminate the foreigners in North China seventy-five years ago. The contemporary youth movement was ordered to wipe out "old ideas, old customs, old habits, old culture," but all the time Mao was condemning the past he seemed unconsciously imprisoned by it.

It is not difficult to hear echoes of Chinese history in the rhetoric of her Marxist leaders. And that should not surprise us. Twenty-five dynasties preceded the present generation of leadership. Hundreds of emperors have ruled from Peking and Mao could not and Teng cannot escape the ghosts of the past. Even when trying to destroy the traditions which they profess to loathe, they are forced to use methods which served other generations of rulers.

This raises the question asked ever since the Communists began to build the so-called new order: "How Marxist is it, and how Chinese?" The ideology may belong to Marx, but the "spirit" is true Chinese.

Take the case of Mao. Founders of dynasties always had to be extraordinary persons—men bigger than life. They had to be both wise and brave, scholarly and paternal. The reign of an emperor was more a personal rule than a dispassionate monarchy. He made judgments and was the arbiter of disputes. Personal loyalty to the ruler was very important. He was not just a number in a dynastic genealogy; he was a superior man whom you knew, albeit remotely.

You will see the face and personality of Chairman Mao in the above description—"the great helmsman" and "the brightest red sun in our hearts"—bigger than life.

He could not escape his past.

Another example of copying the old: The network

of spies and informers in the Chinese Marxist (and Nationalist) systems is straight out of the distant past. Collective reponsibility has been around for a long time in the Middle Kingdom. It simply means that all family members were responsible for each other and neighbors bore the responsibility for their neighboring families. If a family member did wrong and ran away, you had to pay for him. Which meant that you kept an eye on him. The result was that everybody watched everybody else, which beats having to pay to get the job done. It still works that way.

So it seems, as someone said, no matter how much things change, somehow they seem to remain the same.

China Is Still China

So we come to China's newest new day. How different will it be? There are jet planes to be bought, oil to be discovered, cultural exchanges to be made, computer technology to be learned, foreign loans to be approved, clothes to be redesigned, first-class hotels to be built, a communications industry to be updated.

And all the time it's still the Middle Kingdom. China never intends to be weak again. Never again will it be told what to do. Never again will it abdicate its power to another. China will continue to take care of China, just as every other nation looks after its own interests. It will establish its own priorities. It will do what seems right for China. It will not buy what it does not want; it will not recognize whom it does not choose to.

The current rush for things Western will always fill that deeper Chinese purpose: To make a great China even greater; to make a powerful people yet more powerful; to make the Middle Kingdom the most dominant, influential force the world has ever seen. This is something not to be forgotten in the midst of our euphoria over political recognition and the toasts of good cheer being raised on both sides of the Pacific Ocean.

In 1916, Li Ta-chao, a Chinese Marxist wrote: "Grey-haired China has one foot in the grave, while a youthful China is . . . conceived. . . . Now, when things are dying, yet being born; when they are being ruined, yet being completed; destroyed, yet constructed; decaying, yet blossoming . . . every sound evokes an echo, and every echo awakes a dream, so that the self-awakening of each individual leads to the self-awakening of an entire people. Let everyone arise resolutely and march forward courageously without looking back, to demand . . . an ideal China."

This was a powerful prohecy to be spoken at a time of almost total national decay and despair. It also says something for today's China, although it would be false to say that the nation has one foot in the grave. But once again some things are dying, yet being born, and are being destroyed, yet being contructed. Mao's thoughts are no longer unchallenged truth. Every day they are being criticized, reinterpreted and challenged on the wall posters that adorn Peking streets. His dreams are fading, but new dreams are being born.

Ancient Chinese animosities toward the outside world seem to be abating, while a somewhat open appreciation for the West appears to be at hand. Something is being destroyed, yet constructed.

And this much can be stated with certainty: Things will change again, and again, and again.

Parts of this book should be written in pencil because the next political movement could reconstruct everyone's thinking. A purge of the leadership could put Peking onto another course. A renewed xenophobia could compel the Chinese to once again go it alone.

It would be wise to keep our enthusiam over China's new day balanced with a pragmatic recognition of these possibilities. They can all happen because China really hasn't changed that much. China is China, and Peking will do what Peking must do. Chinese-style Marxism is in constant flux, but the words of the ancient sages live on. That's where China ultimately receives nourishment for its spirit whether the leadership admits it or not. Thirty years of Marx have not changed China at the core.

This is not to say that China's new stance toward the West—and toward the United States, in particular—is a devious plot perpetrated by scheming Asians. These new political arrangements bring the world into realistic alignment.

But China is still the Middle Kingdom. And as its military and economic strength increase in the days ahead, its ancient sense of destiny will again and again give it the spirit to carry on.

The challenge to the West is to be strong enough, courageous enough and tough enough to coexist with a country that still somehow believes that a stone in Peking continues to be the center of the world.

3
Will Mao's Thoughts Live On?

To give the throne to another man would be easy; to find a man who shall benefit the kingdom is difficult.

Mencius, 372-289 B.C.

Mao Tse-tung's father owned a small piece of land in Shao Shan, dedicated primarily to the growing of rice. The family lived very simply in their small house on the hillside. Life revolved around the seasonal activities of planting, cultivating and harvesting. The son was certainly out of the loins of his father. Both were stubborn and quarrelsome, never succeeding in coming to an agreement on any subject.

Father Mao sent his eldest son to the small country school in the home province of Hunan. There the boy learned a few Chinese characters and was taught how to count. The father never intended his son to receive any more advanced education because he was needed to help on the farm and they were much too poor to hire a laborer.

However, when the son had mastered characters that enabled him to read simple stories, he came into possession of a novel which he was able to understand to some extent. Very few books were available in the small village where he lived and it happened that the most popularly read were two novels, the *Shui Hu* and the *San Kuo Chih Yen I*. The first recounts the adventures of 108 brigands who had banded together; the second relates the tale of the wars between the Three Kingdoms. Mao Tse-tung became passionately fond of these two books and devoted every possible moment which he could spare from his work on the farm to reading them.

Meanwhile, the young Mao grew very tall and strong. When he reached the age of fourteen or fifteen, he was already as tall and as big as his father who was of sturdy South China peasant stock. The boy could carry on his broad shoulders two of the heavy manure baskets which had to be taken to the fields several times each day.

The father was very happy to have such an efficient helper in his son, but Mao Tse-tung's thoughts were elsewhere. He would take his books with him to the fields every day, and whenever the opportunity arose he would steal away to his favorite hiding place under a tree behind an ancient tomb. Frequently he arrived at a state bordering on ecstasy as he followed, word by word, the lives and adventures of the powerful bandits or read of the schemings and stratagems in the wars of the Three Kingdoms.

Mao Is Caught Red-Handed

His father, whose life was completely wrapped up in the daily routine of the work on the farm, began to notice his son's frequent absences and to worry about the farm work which remained undone. Finally one day he caught young Mao red-handed, sitting behind the tomb with a novel in his hand and the two empty manure baskets.

The father was furious.

An old friend, Siao-Yu, recreated the following conversations between father and son in his book, *Mao and I Were Beggars*.

"So you have decided to stop work, have you?" the father shouted at the son.

"No, Father, I am only having a little rest," his son replied.

"But you have not carried any manure all this whole morning!"

"Oh, yes I have. I have carried several baskets since dawn." The baskets were like those in use all over China—two are carried together, slung one at each end of a pole, and supported like a yoke on the shoulders.

"How many?"

"Five or six at least since dawn."

"Only five or six in half a day? And do you think

53

that is enough to earn your living?"

"Well, and how many do you think you could carry in half a day?"

"Twenty! Or at least fifteen."

"But from the house to the field is a very long way."

"I suppose you think I should build the house right on the edge of the field to make your work lighter! Didn't I have to do just the same when I was a boy your age? It seems you no longer care what happens to your family. How do you think we're going to live? There you sit quite calmly as if you had not a care in the world! Have you no sense of gratitude? What good can it possibly do to waste your time reading those stupid books? You are not a child any more and if you want to eat, you must work!"

"Oh, hush. That's enough. You are always complaining," Mao Tse-tung replied.

After this scene, they went back to the house for lunch. About five o'clock, the youthful Mao disappeared again. This time his father found him easily. He went straight to the old tomb and the sight which had so aroused his wrath in the morning again met his gaze. There his son sat with his book in his hands and the empty baskets beside him. The quarrel which had been interrupted in the morning began again:

"Has your mind been so completely turned by hose bad books that you no longer pay attention to what your father says to you?"

"No, Father. I do listen to you. I do everything you tell me to do."

"You know very well what I want. I want you to give your mind to the farm and to work regularly in the fields, and to read no more of these bad books."

"I will work regularly on the farm, but I want to read my books as well. I promise you I will work in the fields and then I will read afterwards. When I have finished my work in the fields, I am free, am I not? Then you can't complain and scold. If I do my share of the work in the fields, you have no right to stop me from reading my books when my tasks are finished."

"But, my son, you carry just a few baskets and then you come and hide here to read."

"Before I came here to read, I did all that you asked," Mao Tse-tung replied quietly.

"And what was that?" the father demanded.

"After lunch, I have carried fifteen baskets of manure. If you doubt my word, you may go to the field and count them for yourself. Then you may come back here. But please leave me in peace now. I want to read."

His father gazed at Mao Tse-tung in open-mouthed amazement. Fifteen baskets represented really heavy work for half a day, and if his son spoke the truth, he certainly could find no cause for complaint. Baffled and sorrowful at this unusual son of his, he plodded his way to the field where the family was working and counted exactly fifteen baskets.

From that day, Mao Tse-tung read his beloved warrior and bandit novels in peace in his hiding place after he had accomplished the work his father demanded. The routine went on day after day, for his desire to learn was insatiable.

His Day of Manhood

The relationship with his father got worse until there was no relationship at all. The decision that followed was inevitable. He would strike out on his own.

Early the morning of his departure—his first day of manhood—Mao tied his few belongings on both ends of a bamboo pole. On one end he slung a mosquito net, two white sheets and several old, tattered tunics. To the other end of the pole he tied his two precious novels.

His mother, filled with anxiety, watched the preparations silently. When he was ready to go, she asked, "Are you going to say good-bye to your father?"

"No, I am not," answered Mao.

"Do you need anything more to take with you?"

"No, I have everything I need."

The farewell was deliberate and unemotional. He walked out of his old thatched home and strode off down the road, not even turning his head to look back at his old mother standing in the door.

Mao Tse-tung had made up his mind to go to school.

When the robust lad entered the headmaster's office, he repeated in the most respectful voice he could command his request: "Sir, please, will you allow me to study in your school?"

The headmaster looked him up and down, somewhat in disbelief at his size, and asked, "What is your name, boy?"

"My name, sir, is Mao Tse-tung."

"Where do you live, Mao Tse-tung?"

"I live in Shao Shan, about forty or fifty *li* from here."

"And how old are you?"

"I am just a little over fifteen years old, sir."

"You look big enough to be at least seventeen or eighteen years old."

"No, sir, I am just fifteen years and some months old."

"Have you attended your village school?"

"I studied for two years with Mr. Wang and I can read novels quite well."

"Have you read the primary school books?"

"No, sir, I haven't read them."

"Are you able to read the second-year school books?"

"Most of them. There are some words I don't know yet."

"Have you learned any mathematics?"

"No, sir, I haven't."

"How much history and geography do you know?"

"I haven't learned any history or geography yet."

"I want you to write two lines of classic characters."

Mao took the pen and wrote some words in a very clumsy fashion. His hands were large and calloused, much more comfortable around an axe handle than holding a small brush.

"No, it's no good. You cannot come to this school. We have no primary classes for beginners. Besides, you are too big to go to a primary school."

"Oh, please, let me enter your school. I want to study," pleaded the desperate young man.

"You could not follow the classes. It's quite hopeless."

"But I will try. Please let me stay."

"No, that's impossible. You could never follow the classes. It would be a waste of your time."

"But I will try very hard. . . ."

Persistence prevailed. The headmaster relented and Mao was accepted. Finally, he was in school, surrounded with books and learning. It was something he had wanted more than anything else in the world.

The Revolutionary Road

It is said in China that Hunan natives like to boast, *Iao tze pu pa hsieh!* "Me? I'm not afraid of the devil himself." Mao Tse-tung would live up to the reputation of his province.

Throughout the years to follow, Mao would fast become the unforgiving revolutionary. A hatred of his father was perhaps the beginning of Mao's persuasion that the old feudal system was evil. He had seen those evils at close hand and they stuck deep in his soul.

In school, he was abused and laughed at because his arms were longer than his shirt-sleeves. Often it was only his great size that kept his antagonists at bay. Later, as a library assistant at Peking University, he suffered further verbal attacks from university elites. When he tried to make conversation with some of the leading intellectuals, he was rebuffed. They scorned Mao and said they "had no time to listen to an assistant librarian speaking southern dialect."

Once after a university lecture by the respected intellectual, Dr. Hu Shih, Mao tried to ask the famed professor a question. When Professor Hu learned that Mao was not an enrolled student but a mere library assistant, he refused to talk to him. These constant personal attacks embittered him all the more.

But eventually Mao found people to talk to—people who would also listen to him. These men, however, were not among China's conservative elite. Rather they were intellectuals who were prepared to give China the strongest medicine possible to cure the massive ills of the "sick man of Asia." These were men like Li Ta-chao, who had founded the "Marxist Study Group," and Chen Tu-shiu whom Mao later said influenced him "perhaps more than anyone else."

Under Li Ta-chao, Mao says in his autobiography, he "developed rapidly toward Marxism." Mao admits he was "more and more radical" as well as "confused, looking for a road." The more he was snubbed by the academic elite, the more Mao was tempted by outright anarchism. Like so many others of his generation, he was hellbent on destroying every restraint that traditional society had placed on the Chinese people.

Long years of revolutionary struggle followed. During those harsh decades of guerrilla warfare, Mao became more and more convinced of the righteousness of his cause which was nothing less than the salvation of the Chinese people.

He was untiring. He read incessantly, only this time he was not reading about China's warriors of the past. He *was* the warrior. In the caves and in the mountains, Mao was never without his books. He was an admirer of George Washington for the brilliance of his leadership in the American Revolution.

As he read, he also wrote. While others slept, Mao put the next day's strategy on paper. He wrote of the glorious future to be won and of the past from which many things could be learned.

Mao's Thoughts Develop

Slowly, his speeches began to fill volumes. His exhortations stirred the hearts of the common people. His analysis of the rapidly changing scene in China was written down and believed as dogma. His thoughts were quoted, memorized, hand-copied, broadcast and even put to song.

During the Cultural Revolution of 1966, the *Peking Review* wrote, "Singing Chairman Mao's quotations helps us to remember his words. With revolutionary hearts serving the people, we throw away self-interest and promote the public good for the sake of the revolution. . . . While we sing these new songs, a red sun rises in our hearts."

But what of those prolific thoughts? Will they stand the stress of changing events? Will they compete for a place in history with the wisdom of China's ancient sages?

The answer is a good Middle Kingdom response. Probably yes and probably no. Some thoughts have a Confucian ring to them. They will likely survive. Other quotations were only of immediate value. Mao's famous "little red book" seems to have been edited to stimulate his followers to maintain revolutionary purity. Semi-Confucian in nature, much of the content was a blend of homespun Chinese homilies and biblical axioms. Many are demonstrably true, but their long-term significance is purely in the mind of the reader.

Poor and Blank

In 1958 Mao wrote, "China's 600 million people have two remarkable peculiarities; they are, first of all, poor and secondly, blank. That may seem like a bad thing, but it is really a good thing. Poor people want change, want to do things, want revolution. A clean sheet of paper has no blotches, and so the newest and most beautiful words can be written on it, the newest and most beautiful pictures can be painted on it."

This will probably be true for a few more years to come. China in 1979 is still a tremendously poor country. Visitors who have recently traveled to the interior say that the revolution has scarcely touched some regions. Mao would still insist, perhaps, that this poverty is essentially a good thing. The rumblings being heard throughout the land, however, indicate that the Chinese peasantry may have tuned out the "great helmsman's" romantic view of their condition. They have heard of a better life and seem eager to become a part of it.

Mao's second point—that it is good the Chinese are "blank"—may also be less true today than it was twenty-one years ago. China is more literate today than in all its previous history. Throughout China's years of isolation the British Broadcasting Corporation, Voice of America, Far East Broadcasting Company and other international shortwave radio signals have found their way into Chinese hearts and minds. Regular visits from Hong Kong mothers, fathers, cousins and grandchildren have told the Chinese of the good life outside, in the world of freedom. They have not forgotten.

While 80 percent of the Chinese are still farmers, they are no longer illiterate peasants. Along with the nation, they, too, have stood up. Mao taught them that "to rebel is justified" and they may just decide to do it again. No more can the Chinese be seen through the misty eyes of a Mao as a people who are like "a clean sheet of paper that has no blotches."

New characters have been written on those pages. Many are filled with smudges. Some have been crossed out. And still others carry messages that contradict some of Mao's basic doctrines.

Paper Tigers and the Masses

The "little red book" reminded the people that "All reactionaries are paper tigers. In appearance, the reactionaries are terrifying, but in reality they are not so powerful. From a long-term view, it is not the reactionaries, but the people who are really powerful."

This bit of hyperbole is not out of character for Mao. In his book, *Mao Tse-tung*, Stuart Schram observes that Mao tended to exercise a ". . . progressive exaltation of the human will over the rational analysis of the facts."

In other words, Mao knew the power of the enemy's destructive weapons and had an honest fear of what they could do. But even in the face of this, Mao continued to put the Chinese masses against all obstacles. He wrote: "We must have faith in the masses and we must have faith in the Party. These are two cardinal principles. If we doubt these principles, we shall accomplish nothing."

He never doubted the strength of the Chinese people. Even though the paper tigers had nuclear teeth, his study of revolution had taught him that it was the masses who moved the world. It was the masses who fought uncompromisingly for their cause.

"I have witnessed the tremendous energy of the masses," he said. "On this foundation it is possible to accomplish any task whatsoever."

Mao really believed it, but that didn't necessarily make it so. Even within China, many skeptics felt that too much emphasis was placed on the ominiscience of man's will in Mao's thought. And not only that, but also the alleged perfectibility of the human spirit. Some of Mao's detractors said—quietly, to be sure—that to give the masses credit for everything was more conducive to building national *esprit de corps* than to building a modern economy.

It appears that Chairman Hua Kuo-feng and Vice Premier Teng Hsiao-p'ing are now saying this aloud. Undoubtedly, today's leadership sees the masses of China as a mixed blessing. When they look at the masses they see something more than political ideology. Eighteen million more mouths to feed each year, for instance, in a country so poor that most are just barely receiving an adequate diet. Plus the need for houses, health care and jobs.

For the new pragmatists, China's millions are a bittersweet fact of economic and social life.

As change comes, however, and if China moves successfully toward its goal of full modernization by the year 2000, the masses will have begun to receive some of those benefits personally. Further, if China continues to develop its nuclear defense to the degree where the Soviets would not dare attack, then the country may get the breathing room it needs to become a major industrial power by the turn of the century.

Today the "poor, blank" Chinese masses are a little threat. But a billion well-fed, well-armored, well-educated Chinese will be a force to reckon with.

A Toned-Down Revolution

Mao once said, "It is necessary to train and bring up millions of successors who will carry on the cause of the proletarian revolution." He freely admitted that after he left the scene, the revolution might or might not succeed. It would depend on the spirit of the successors.

But ever since his death in 1976, there has been almost no momentum for recruitment. The drive for successors has slowed to a walk.

The Chinese are tired of movements. It is the only thing most have ever known. Chinese youth want to learn physics, not politics. Girls want to have their hair done in beauty parlors and wear brightly colored clothes. They've had enough of khaki. The new regime still needs its soldiers and politicians, party bosses and cadre leaders. But not everyone wants to be a revolutionary leader. Whereas Mao would have the students retreat to the countryside "to attack the capitalist roaders," that same student now wants to go to Stanford or Harvard or the University of Peking.

A lot of them would settle for even the local trade school.

Mao once wrote, "How should we judge whether a youth is a revolutionary? How can we tell? There is only one criterion, namely whether or not he is willing to integrate himself with the broad masses of workers and peasants and does so in practice."

If that is so then the revolution is in trouble. Modern Chinese youth are thinking more of themselves than they are the broad masses. It is these better educated, more sophisticated groups of Chinese youth who are helping to slow the revolution. Recruits are down. Old ways have once again started to set in.

What we see in China today is a long way from the frenzy of the Cultural Revolution. During the height of that violent movement, a "liberated" Chinese woman was seen painting these lines on the wall of her factory's mess hall:

The machine is my husband,
The factory is my family.
The fruits of my labor are my children,
The Party is my mother and father.

You won't see revolutionary poetry like that on the walls of China any more. The posters now have messages like "We want more contacts with Americans" and "More human rights for imprisoned political prisoners."

China is still China and it will always be. But it is becoming less and less Maoist. It is still a land of revolution, but the Maoist edge has been taken off. If a vote were taken in China today between who wants to be "red" and who wants to be "expert," it wouldn't even be a race.

Mao once said, "Let 100 flowers blossom, let 100 schools of thought contend." It seems that he later regretted that particular bit of philosophy since he nipped some of the blossoms just as they were beginning to bud. Today the blooms appear—flowers of limited cultural exchange, a controlled foreign presence, a respite in revolutionary rhetoric, more freedom to study basic courses in school, increased freedom of personal expression.

Mao had likely already given his tentative blessing to some of these moves, but the speed with which they are happening today would surprise, and perhaps shock, the author of the "little red book."

Political Work Sidetracked

In 1933, Mao wrote, "Political work is the lifeline of economic work. This is particularly true at a time when the economic and social system is undergoing a fundamental change." China today is going through some profound economic and social change, but is the political work being done? Has this thought of Mao already been laid aside?

If the political work is being attended to, it is certainly less radical than we've seen in the past. Contrary to Mao's explicit command, it appears that serious political work is being shelved, at least for now. In its place, China is using the national energy to seek the expertise it so desperately needs from the West.

For the most part, the expected increase in trade with the West will be for the specific purpose of building a more solid industrial base. The Chinese people themselves will get a few selected consumer items from the West—Coca-Cola, Big Macs and some designs by Pierre Cardin. But they will still have to wait a long time for their own form of the "good life."

Some will wait patiently; others may not. The West and its "things" have always been the world's greatest subverters of revolution. Mao knew this and that's one reason why he fought to keep the West at arm's length. Teng Hsiao-p'ing is not ignorant of it either, but he doesn't seem to care.

Mao and Confucius both applauded austerity.

Mao was happy that the Chinese were "poor and blank." Confucius praised a frugal disciple. The sage once said, "Worthy indeed was Hui! A single bamboo bowl of millet to eat, a gourdful of water to drink, living in a back alley—others would have found it unendurably depressing, but Hui's cheerfulness was not affected at all. Worthy indeed was Hui!"

That might appeal to some aesthetic Chinese, but most of the people are sure to choose the consumer society over the austerity of politics.

Sloganeering as Politics

Mao's rule was synonymous with slogans. While the sloganeering has continued, the Maoist abstract messages ("Take class struggle as the key link") have given way to goal-oriented pragmatism ("Make greater contributions to the Four Modernizations").

Artistic expression that does not conform to the earlier stereotyped model is now being tolerated. The Canton Philharmonic plays Liszt. It's still revolutionary China, but it is revolution in three-quarter time.

During the heat of the mid-sixties' Cultural Revolution, Mao Tse-tung told a group of Red Guards that the revolution was in their hands. If it succeeded, he said, it would be because of them. If it didn't, they would also be the reason. It was reported that Mao wept as he spoke.

One wonders if he would have tears for the

redirection of his revolution today? A *Time* magazine correspondent comments: "A few years ago, if a farmer were asked about the most important factor in increasing rice production, he would answer automatically, 'Mastering the thought of Chairman Mao.' Now he is more likely to respond, 'More chemical fertilizer.'"

The quotations of the Chairman no longer appear in the upper right hand corner of the front page of the *People's Daily*. In March, 1978, the Chinese press stopped printing all Mao quotes in bold type. Not so slowly, the former dogma of Mao Tse-tung is being eroded away.

The "little red book" is long gone. His larger *Selected Works* lies gathering dust.

Mao's Place in History

Mao has been credited with saying that the ultimate victory between socialism and capitalism will not be decided overnight. "Several decades won't do it," he said. "Success requires anywhere from one to several centuries." He is certainly right. But at the same time, since both systems are dynamic rather than static, neither is apt to remain exactly what it is today.

Discussing a territorial dispute in 1978, Teng told a Japanese delegation in Tokyo, "Let's put it off for ten or twenty years. After all, who knows what kind of system we'll have?"

Score one for Teng. The changes in both types of

systems may be a part of our political future shock.

Mao Tse-tung and former Premier Chou En-lai both subscribed to making China a "fully modern socialist state" by the year 2000. Mao pounded at this theme. He thought it could happen by keeping the revolution pure through periodic purges and social upheaval. But the present leadership in Peking wisely chose not to rely solely on ideology and "motivated peasants" to speed China toward that goal. Mao may have seen the new "reliance on the West" as inevitable, and in the wisdom of his final years may even have given it his tacit support. His death, however, seems to have removed any final obstacles to China's rush to the West for technological help.

O. Edmund Clubb, former director of Chinese affairs in the U.S. State Department, wrote in *Current History* that after Mao's death, China's new leaders "undertook fundamental revisions in the realm of domestic affairs; ideology and practice alike were turned around in industry, agriculture and education, sometimes 180 degrees, to be given a more pragmatic thrust."

The question we all ask is, "Will the momentum continue?" Will the spirit of Mao's revolution live on, if not his thoughts? The thoughts of Chairman Mao will probably recede as the man himself is further demythologized. History will always remember him as the great revolutionary leader who was the creator of modern China. Nothing can take that niche away from him.

But continued criticism—especially of his excesses—will make his quotes less quotable.

Mao's Six Achievements

A respected London newspaper, *The Economist,* outlined what it felt were the six main achievements during the reign of Mao:

1. Avoidance of enslavement by the Soviet Union.

2. Attainment of rural full employment.

3. Establishment of a "working man's welfare system" in the towns so that every Chinese can buy his basic rations (overcrowded housing, adequate but unexciting food, a Mao suit a year and cooking oil) for an incredibly cheap two dollars per person a week.

4. Creation of a public health system that has rasied the life expectancy from thirty years in 1949 to about sixty years now.

5. Institution of a practical education for most Chinese children up to age fifteen, and by the 1980s probably up to age seventeen for most.

6. Virtual abolition of violent crime.

That it was all done with the shedding of a great deal of blood and the repression of most human rights goes without saying.

History has already begun its judgment of Mao and his judgment before God will come later. Neither of those, however, will alter the achievements in China. To carry on these programs, however, the Chinese will not need the thoughts or the rhetoric of a Chairman Mao. Instead, they will need sober minds and realistic financial planning. And the Chinese have the full capability for both.

The country will move ahead even as Mao recedes. His thoughts have been the orthodox scriptures for all modern Chinese. It is all most have known. Anything contradictory was heresy. But in the new order it is permissible—within bounds—to revise, rewrite or remove those secular truths which came from the mouth of China's great revolutionary.

The trend, it seems safe to predict, will continue.

The stolid and stubborn fifteen-year-old who used to fight with his father down on the farm is now quickly fading in the face of the emergence of that bigger struggle—bringing China to its rightful place among nations. Some say Mao lived too long. Perhaps. But there is no doubt that his imprint will be on his land and on his people for generations yet to come.

His thoughts may recede into history, but the presence of the man will remain.

China will always be China. Mao's brief dynasty, its seems, has come to an end.

4
There's a China in Your Future

We have no eternal allies and we have no perpetual enemies. Our interests are eternal and those interests it is our duty to follow.
Lord Palmerston

China could be reached, I was told as a boy, by digging straight down, but I never tried it. It wasn't because I doubted what I was told, but because I had no special desire at that time to go to China.

Probably I was not alone. It was quite impossible for me to conceive that a society half-a-world away—straight down—was important to my own interests and aspirations.

I might have felt differently about it if I had known more about our past and could have anticipated more about their future. The fact is that the destinies of China and the United States have been intertwined since even before the American Revolution. Did you know, for example, that without China there might not have been a Boston

Tea Party? What the American revolutionaries dumped into Boston harbor—to protest King George's tax—was a shipload of tea from Amoy, the South China port that faces Taiwan.

As both great powers approached the twenty-first century their destinies seem to be linked even closer. The establishment of full diplomatic relations between Washington and Peking could change forever the way our two peoples regard each other. As Linda Mathews, Hong Kong correspondent for the *Los Angeles Times*, puts it: "Normalization does not imply a new Sino-American alliance, but it does mean the two countries now approach each other as equals, as trade partners and, perhaps, despite the ideological differences that remain, as prospective allies."

When President Carter made his dramatic announcement on December 15, 1978, there was speculation that he was trying to bring pressure to bear on the Soviet Union to complete the long-stalled agreement on strategic arms limitation. However, the president told the nationwide television audience: "We do not undertake this important step for transient tactical or expedient reasons. In recognizing that the government of the People's Republic is the single government of China, we are recognizing simple reality."

It was inevitable that the two great world powers should extend the hand of cooperation to each other. Certainly it was abnormal that mainland China had lived for nearly thirty years in self-imposed isolation. Often the question was asked: "How long can one-fourth of the world's people be kept locked away from the rest of humanity?"

In answer to the question, Asians would tell you the story of the continent's greatest natural resource, bamboo. It is found everywhere. A farmer lives in a bamboo house, sits on bamboo chairs and eats food prepared in bamboo containers. His bed is a bamboo mat. He wears sandals woven from bamboo strips. Bamboo cages hold his chickens and pigs, and a bamboo fence encloses his yard. Bamboo provides shade, and tender young bamboo sprouts are eaten. Rafts, sails, tow rope and tools are fashioned out of bamboo.

China is like the bamboo, Asians will tell you. Omnipresent and resilient. Storms may bend it double, but the bamboo swings back when the wind blows in another direction.

"You Westerners worry too much," I was told. "Don't fret. China will correct her ills someday. It may take a generation. Perhaps longer. But like a giant bamboo swinging left and right, China will swing back to normal eventually."

All the current signs confirm their confidence. The bamboo is righting itself. Even the little indicators point to it. Things like taxi service in Peking. With only a bit of tongue-in-cheek, diplomatic residents say that the length of time you wait for a taxi is the surest way to measure your country's standing with the Chinese. When you call the Capital Taxi Service, they first ask your nationality before telling you how long you must wait for the taxi to arrive.

"Americans used to have to wait an hour," one young diplomat said. "If we were in a hurry, we would claim to be Albanians."

But with normalization of Sino-American relations, taxis began to appear within moments for waiting American customers. Because the Albanian government criticized China for taking the "capitalist road," it is now Albanian diplomats who are left standing.

The most telling evidence that a degree of normalcy has arrived, however, is the number of Chinese citizens who are applying for immigration visas to the United States. It used to be that even the thought of emigrating—if voiced—could get you a knock on the door at midnight. With the announcement of diplomatic recognition, applications jumped almost overnight from 100 a month to 1,000 in December, 1978. The authorities seemed to be letting anyone leave who could prove that he had relatives overseas.

For many that was not difficult. There are an estimated forty-two million Chinese who live off the mainland. The major concentrations are in Taiwan, Hong Kong and Singapore, but Chinese are the merchants and shopkeepers in virtually every other Asian country as well, except Japan and South

Korea. Many are second- and third-generation families in the country where they live, but for hosts of them links to the homeland are still strong.

The United States has a Chinese population of about 675,000. The ancestral home for most of them was in Kwangtung province so it is not surprising that the sudden surge of eager emigrants is felt principally in that area which borders Hong Kong. The relaxed attitude of the Peking government regarding exit permits is based on "humanitarian grounds," the *Peking Daily* says, and is an effort to reunite families who have been separated for long periods of time.

Look Who's Coming to Study

For most of us, however, our contact with Chinese people will not be through relatives, but with tourists and students. There will be considerably more of the latter than the former. China is more interested in having tourists come to the Middle Kingdom—because they bring foreign exchange—than in allowing their people to travel outside the country purely for tourism. Incoming tourists bring money while outgoing ones take it away, and China needs all the dollars she can get to pay for the massive modernization program.

But of students abroad there will be plenty. The Peking government has announced its intention to send 20,000 scholars to foreign colleges and universities by 1985 and indicated they might actually double that number. Most of them will come to the United States, and they will be China's best, pursuing primarily postgraduate work and research. After spending a few months brushing up on the English language, they will turn their attention to such fields as physics, optical science, molecular biology, chemical engineering and other scientific pursuits.

This could prove to be a most interesting encounter. When thirty-year-old Mr. Wang comes to do research in engineering at the university in your city, he will be a man who probably was a teen-age Red Guard during China's violent Cultural Revolution. He may have been part of an organized demonstration which denounced technicians and teachers for studying science and human behavior instead of making revolution. Time has moderated his views, but chances are he still has unresolved questions that trouble him.

Miss Li, the polite and demure twenty-five-year-old who comes to do graduate studies in computer technology at Stanford, may have been one of those elementary school children who, during recess, would throw rocks at a stuffed caricature of Uncle Sam, shouting, *"Ta tao ti kuo chu i!"*—"Down with American imperialism!" She, too, is likely to have residual feelings inside which she cannot—or will not—articulate.

How we respond to these visitors whose childhoods were manipulated by the Party and for the Party could play a major role in future relationships between the two countries. Our attitudes toward them might even help shape the future direction of China. Former Premier Chou En-lai and the present Vice Premier Teng Hsiao-p'ing were once students in France. China is what it is today at least partially because, by Chou's and Teng's own testimony, their radical beliefs were nourished in French universities.

The student who now is studying in your city may be the leader who takes China into the twenty-first century. What an opportunity to engage in our own personal one-to-one "people diplomacy."

A burden for prayer and witness is already felt among many Chinese Christian student groups which exist on university campuses across the United States. Perhaps more than anyone, these ABC (American-born Chinese) students who are Christians will have fantastic opportunities to relate to their ethnic cousins as they seek to adjust to the strangeness of a totally different culture.

The Shock of Western Culture

If Christians do not make opportunities for them to be exposed to some of America's deeper values, the materialistic and hedonistic excesses of Western culture could have serious negative impacts on these Chinese students who have grown up in an environment where personal behavior is carefully regulated and where personal ambition is sublimated for the greater good of society.

Chinese Communism may have oppressed, imprisoned and even killed many of its citizens, but its insistence on spartan living, sexual morality and service to the people has given a virtual puritan character to the country.

Mrs. Billy Graham, who grew up in China as the daughter of missionaries, expresses deep concern that the pornography, idolatry and violence of a supposedly Christian nation "may convince many of these students that atheistic communism is at least as good, and perhaps preferable, to godless materialism."

Already the *People's Daily* is getting Chinese citizens ready for exposure to the glaring differences between the two countries. In a series of seven articles, the Peking paper reported the impressions of a group of Chinese journalists who in late 1978 spent three weeks traveling in the United States. It was frank, objective reporting and the Chinese newsmen did not attempt to disguise the affluence of most Americans in a consumer-oriented society which the Chinese claim to disdain.

Neither did they omit warts on the capitalistic face. As one news magazine observed, " . . . the end result was a surprising mosaic of the good and seamy sides of America."

The writers commented that "Americans have accomplished many things that are worth learning. Of course, the life style of a capitalist society cannot be separated from debauchery. It is unfair, however, to look at only this aspect. The Americans are famous for their efficiency. When they are working, they are diligent and tense. When they work, they work. When they play, they play. . . . There is no idle person and no idle conversation."

"There are, of course, some pleasure-oriented men and women among American young people," one article said, "but there are also many who study strenuously and work diligently. . . . A kind American driver took us in his car to see the other side of New York. . . . These are the slums. . . . On Broadway, the driver pointed out to us some places where X-rated movies and strip dances were shown. He also asked us to notice the prostitutes on the street."

But the bad was balanced by the good: "The Americans are not . . . content with the status quo. In this exceedingly competitive capitalist society, whoever does not seek technological progress will perish. Although their technological level is equal to the highest in the world, they do not refuse to learn from foreign countries."

The series concluded: "We should learn the good points of advanced capitalist countries and at the same time screen out all the corrupt things. We should learn their science, but at the same time should reject their philosophy. . . . Since we have the superior social system, we should be able to avoid the evils of capitalism."

Whether or not the Chinese students who are here and those who are coming reject our philosophy, as the *People's Daily* advises, we should fervently pray they will be discerning and mature enough to "screen out all the corrupt things" and see our heritage of faith in God, which is at the heart of America's greatness.

Youth and the Family

Family life in China has not had an easy time of it during the past thirty years. The Communist threat to this fundamental building block of the Chinese social order has probably been the single greatest contributing factor to national unease and mental distress. For centuries, the closely knit Chinese family has provided the foundation for all national life. So basic has been this structure that the word for country is *gwo jya*—literally, a "nation of families."

Historically, family relationships were so intricately worked out that the social system and the family system were inseparable. The family unit was at the heart of everything. Every child, every adult had a sense of place. His or her position in Chinese society was directly tied to his unquestioned, unalterable position within the family.

The father's authority was absolute. Females were subordinate to males. Older brothers held rank over younger siblings. Youth gave way to age, inexperience to wisdom. Marriages were arranged to fit the system.

This is the way it had always been. Only the very brave—or the very foolish—would dare question the wisdom of the arrangement. When there was no political security, the family at least had each other. When the guns roared, when tyrants ravaged the land, when nature ran amok, when the food ran out, the family—that strongest, most invulnerable unit in China—remained intact.

Not all of China's rulers had been happy that greater allegiance was given to the family and the clan than to the nation. The Chinese family had been a major target for reformers during China's modern era. Many of those changes were brought about by China's increasing association with the West. After the revolution of 1912, there were more and more direct attacks on the family and on family loyalties.

Thus when the Communists came to power, the stage had already been set for a final assault on this fortress of Chinese life. It remained only for those who sought the new order to employ their scientific, thorough and uncompromising methods. The Communists knew how. One of the regime's earliest ploys was to transfer private agriculture into collective farms. No longer would a family be responsible for its own plot of land. Father and son would no longer work the land of their ancestors.

As this pattern took over China, family ties were weakened. The individual family no longer held control of the means of production, and the family was atomized still further. The government established nursery schools and homes for the aged, thus taking away an important social function from the family. The all-powerful state would now care for people. What was made to appear as a benevolent move by the Party was actually another blow at the family.

Further, with the young and the old now cared for, the state could impose even greater demands on the adults in the family to produce more for the Revolution. Slowly and inexorably, allegiance once given to the family was transferred to the state.

Struggle between the generations, not their unity which had served the old Chinese society, was to be the basis of the new Marxist order. It was a deliberate, diabolical plot. The cardinal Confucian virtue known as "filial piety" had no place in the People's Republic.

So to destroy the old and bring forth the new, the Communists created something which had never before existed in China—a generation gap. Since the concept was unknown in Chinese society, they also had to create a word for it—*dye go*, literally, "generation moat."

They may have been too successful, for the gap has now become a giant chasm. It was widened and deepened by the Cultural Revolution, which took place between 1966 and 1969 and was, by all odds, the most dramatic and violent organized battle between generations in human history. The effects of that spasm will be felt for a long time.

Today, China's youth can be roughly divided into two groups—and they have both become disillusioned. They are the "materialists" and the "idealists." The latter group is smaller and, perhaps, the most embittered. In addition to possessing the normal idealism of youth, they still carry Mao's dream of a perfect, classless and utopian society. They know that Teng Hsiao-p'ing, with his pragmatism, has tarnished Mao's bright vision and they don't like it. They are angered because the "noble" goals for which they fought in the Cultural Revolution have been scrapped for the Four Modernizations.

These idealists feel that youth should be in control of the Party apparatus, but they know the old will continue to dominate China's future. They are a highly volatile element in a seething society and represent a potent threat to the Great Leap Outward.

The larger group, the "materialists," are likewise restless, but for different reasons. They would like to have not only international relations, but their lives as well, normalized. They would just like to get back to the university or carry on with their job without the constant spoon-feeding of Marxism-Leninism. Their goals are modest—normal family life cushioned by a few creature comforts, but even these things still seem out of reach. If Teng's government cannot provide the minimal consumer items for which they have raised the expectation level, this group could also spell trouble.

Nearly 40 percent of the Chinese people—400 million, or nearly twice the total population of the United States—are under eighteen years of age.

The direction they decide to take and the group they decide to follow will determine the shape of China's future. It could be a return to traditional values within the secure framework of the family. Or it could be a violent eruption which would sweep away the tentative gains made by the new regime and put the country through another period of revolutionary madness.

Pray for China's youth and for their families, because your future and that of your children could be woven inextricably into the strands of their own destiny.

A Nation of Farmers

Most of the families in China—about 80 percent, in fact—still live down on the farm and in small villages. The country, for all its industrialization, remains basically agrarian, and agriculture will remain the first priority for a long time to come. For although a majority of the people are concentrated in food production, output still lags severely behind the critical demands. Part of the reason is the collectivization of land and and labor. Teng Hsiao-p'ing has long seen this weakness and is now using his position to return some of the land to private cultivation. This is not merely revisionist socialism, but a return to a measure of outright capitalism and it was in this connection that Teng made his now famous statement about not caring whether the cat is black or white "as long as it catches mice."

The difficulty of feeding 25 percent of the world's population with only 7 percent of the world's arable land cannot be overstated. Nineteen seventy-eight marked the third successive year when grain output failed to keep pace with population growth. The problem is compounded by the fact that most of the Chinese fields are still tilled by hand. As a result, production per acre is much less than in the United States and Europe. It is even considerably behind Taiwan which ranks near the top in per acre yield.

And because it has limited cash reserves, China is faced with the cruel dilemma of spending its money for either imported grain to feed the people or for equipment and fertilizers to raise food production. They cannot afford to do both at the level necessary, and yet both must be done.

American farmers and farm machinery manufacturers have a big stake in China's future—and she in theirs. In 1978, Peking purchased $500 million worth of wheat and corn from U.S. farmers. Previously, because of political differences with the U.S.A., Australia and Canada had been the big suppliers.

Although China has made no commitment on the purchase of farm machinery, an experiment introduced in 1978 has received rave reports in the Chinese press. In mid-1978, Peking purchased one million dollars worth of John Deere equipment. The collective farm where it was used for six months boosted soybean production by 20 percent and corn yields by 70 percent over the previous year. Each farmer was able to cultivate an average of 165 acres with the modern equipment, about 100 times more than with hand labor and traditional methods.

Since the Chinese are already maximally using such techniques as double-cropping, inter-cropping and intensive hand cultivation, the next quantum jump in production must come from mechanization and the use of chemical fertilizers.

Peking's present shopping list for agricultural products includes fertilizer, herbicides and pesticides, breeding livestock, small farm tools (for the terraced fields south of Peking) and food processing and canning equipment. Machinery is likely to be added later as the money becomes available.

It is not only in our economic interest to help China with her food needs. It seems to be in our political interest as well, for a billion hungry Chinese are likely to be more dangerous than the same number reasonably well-fed.

The Need for Technicians

Until China can train its own technicians and managers, officials say they are ready to hire foreign experts to advise and even help manage existing and future enterprises. Chinese-Americans will be high on the list of people Peking will try to recruit. There is no shortage of them in the U.S., for an incredibly large percentage of Chinese-American young people acquire a university education and are presumably qualified for many of these positions.

It goes without saying that the opportunity for Christians to apply for these openings is unparalleled.

Contracts are also being signed with foreign firms to build and manage huge projects. The only restraint at this point seems to be China's severe shortage of capital, a problem which can be solved only over a period of years. In the meantime, Peking's new government is seeking huge credits—$1.2 billion from Great Britain and undisclosed but even greater amounts from the U.S., France and Japan. It is a decidedly revolutionary move for the Communist regime.

Even more revolutionary, however, is the "equity participation" arrangements which the Chinese say will be allowed in some industries. This would permit foreign investors to put money into Chinese enterprises with the totally capitalistic motive of making a profit—a plan which is certain to be very attractive to hundreds of overseas Chinese investors who have no shortage of the capital Peking needs.

There is even private talk in Hong Kong that Peking officials have hinted at permitting up to 49 percent foreign ownership of joint ventures and guaranteeing—if you can believe this!—that foreign managers would have complete authority in the day-to-day operations. Someone has remarked that this would give overseas companies "more freedom in China than in many non-Communist nations."

All these capitalistic plans by China's socialist rulers have enormous advantages to a country which has so far to go and so little money to take it there. They would give China the factories and plants she needs together with the technical expertise and management capabilities, with a minimum expenditure of her own capital. If you don't care whether the money is red or green—any more than it matters whether the mice-catching cat is black or white—nobody could ask for more than that.

In the year of China's Great Leap Outward, a group of Americans were being guided through a drill-bit factory in Shanghai. A Chinese official accompanying them paused in front of a pile of newly finished drill bits. Then he confided to the visitors: "Yours are better than ours. We want drill bits from you."

Drill bits and a whole lot more.

So many commercial and technological agreements will be signed in the next two or three years that the economic futures of the two nations will be crucially linked for the next twenty-five to fifty years.

If China has not miscalculated the distance to be

covered in its latest leap, a great many existing international political and economic alignments will be reviewed in the years to come—and quite possibly changed.

That could make a big difference in everybody's future.

To Know and Understand

For a country that will so strongly influence our future, most Americans know very little about China. What we do know consists of largely ill-defined generalities, a mixture of fact and fantasy. Alexander Pope gave good counsel when he said:

> A little learning is a dang'rous thing;
> Drink deep, or taste not the Pierian spring:
> There shallow draughts intoxicate the brain,
> And drinking largely sobers us again.

To drink of the Chinese spring can be an intoxicating experience, especially if we restrict ourselves to "shallow draughts." Our fleeting and casual fascination will turn to real understanding only if we will invest the time and accept the discipline of a deeper study of this ancient and intriguing land.

To so immerse ourselves is to taste a culture spanning fifty centuries—of dynasty after dynasty—of kingdoms rising and falling. A culture of prehistoric folk heroes like Fu Hsi who supposedly invented writing, fishing and trapping—and Shen Nung, inventor of trade, commerce and agriculture.

To drink deeply of China means to wade into the philosophical mazes of Confucius, Mo Tzu, Lao Tzu and Mencius—men who tried to steer the sturdy ship of state on a straight, ethical course.

It is a culture of the Great Wall and great men—powerful rulers and fearless defenders of a land which they called the Celestial Kingdom. To understand China is to drink deeply of her poetry and arts. The T'ang (718-907 A.D.) was the golden age of Chinese poetry, where classical verse reached its apex. It was poetry of nature—of man's relationship with mountains, forests and rivers.

A poet of the T'ang, Liu Tsung-yuan, wrote this touching piece:

For a long time I was bound by official cares,
Then suddenly I was banished to the far south,
To dwell at leisure among farmers and fruit growers.
By chance I became a guest of the hills and forests.

This volume is only a "sip" of China. It cannot be more, but is my hope and prayer that some will be stimulated by it to drink deeper. The church needs students and scholars who will devote a lifetime to the study and application of all acquired skills for the sake of the gospel of Jesus Christ in China. God has never been out of China since His name and message were taken there many centuries ago. It is my firm conviction that we will see before the Second Coming of Jesus Christ a mighty breakthrough of God's Spirit in that dry and thirsty land.

It could happen soon. Some of the exciting events of our time could be God's preparation. A Chinese friend of mine has said, "Although political, physical and psychological barriers have been created through Communism, the more difficult barriers of traditional ancestor worship, Confucianism, superstition, rigid adherence to religious customs and, above all, language, have been broken down."

He then asks this question, "Is God plowing the land for the seed to be sown?"

I do not know how it will happen or whom He will use. I just believe that George Müller was right when he said, "Get your tools ready and God will give you work."

The first step for those who would know and understand China in order to be available for God's call is to enroll in Chinese studies and Chinese language. Language is the first tool to put in your hand. Or to use another metaphor, it is the bucket that will allow you to drink deeply of that spring.

More people speak Mandarin than any other language in the world, including English. Yet only a relative handful of Americans who are not of Chinese extraction speak it. Fewer still are studying it, and you could probably number on your two hands those who are learning it as a skill to be used in the work of Jesus Christ among one-fourth of the world's people.

With some distress, I raised the question: "Will the church be ready when God is ready?"

China figures very significantly in the church's past. But God is not just the God of history. He is also the God of the future and because that is true, I believe China is in the church's future.

I must now address a question to you personally: "Is China—somehow, someway, sometime—in *your* future?"

5
The Sages of Ancient China

I do not know whether I was then a man dreaming I was a butterfly, or whether I am now a butterfly dreaming I am a man.

Chuang Tzu, 369-286 B.C.

The history and practice of religion in China differ profoundly from anything we have ever known in our Western experience. One of the reasons the substance of Chinese religion is difficult for us to understand is that what we presume to be religion is often not religion at all. Instead, for the most part, it is a body of philosophical thought, taught and propagated by ancient sages to whom we—in later years—have tended to give theological status.

The misunderstanding is understandable. We've grown up hearing Confucian proverbs like, "Do not do to others what you do not want done to you." It has a religious ring to it, and even sounds like Jesus, except Jesus spoke His Golden Rule in the positive, not the negative. It is these similarities that lead us to make the inaccurate "religious" judgment. If the Bible and Confucius sound so much alike, we reason, then Confucius must have been trying to do what Jesus came to do.

But to argue in this fashion—from the specific to the general—is to miss the point. Confucius never regarded himself as any kind of "savior," nor did he have much to say to his disciples about the afterlife. His sole concern was to reflect the wisdom and truth of China's earlier sages, a theme that stressed the need for man to maintain a "sageliness within and a kingliness without." Further, in the mind of Confucius, the essence of truth was the establishment of a proper order of relationships.

We will see again and again that what Confucius taught and practiced was not "religion," but the most exalted form of humanism. It is this humanistic Chinese mind that has produced the China we know today—a China that is still more Confucian than Marxist.

It has been correctly observed that philosophy has more meaning to the average Chinese than to any other civilization in our world's history. It has seldom mattered to a Chinese whether or not he was religious, but he knew he had to be philosophical—or at least have a rudimentary understanding of fundamental philosophical principles. To understand this Chinese attitude will make us better prepared to hear what China's ancient sages had to say.

Historically, the study of philosophy in China has been the first priority in the educational system. Even in ancient times, if a man had any learning, he would seek it first in philosophy. When children started to school, the first assignment was to begin memorizing the philosophical texts of China's ancients—*The Four Books* of Confucius, the *Book of Mencius*, the *Doctrine of the Mean* and the *Great Learning*.

The first assignment in reading was the so-called *Three Characters Classic* which opened with this statement: "The nature of man is originally good." Again, to the Chinese this was not so much a religious statement as a philosophical one—that elevated man to the highest order of humanism. It was the first truth learned, a truth they would build their lives on and pass on to their children in the best of the Chinese humanistic tradition.

Three Ways to One Goal

While Confucianism has been indisputably the single greatest influence on the culture of China, it has not been the only philosophical force. Without attempting to do the impossible here—outline the history of Chinese philosophical thought—we will briefly consider the three ways of thought that have had the greatest influence on the Chinese throughout their long history—Confucianism, Taoism and Buddhism.

The scholars were Confucian, for the most part,

whereas the *lao pai hsing*—the common people—worshiped randomly at Buddhist monasteries and Taoist temples. The average Chinese saw little, if any, difference between the Buddhist symbols of worship and the indigenous gods of China's hills and rivers.

We cannot conceive of, say, a Presbyterian atheist. But it was no problem for a Chinese to be Confucian, Taoist and Buddhist—if not at the same time, at least espousing each form at some time in his life. (Scholars who lived their lives as Confucianists would often live out their last days in the quiet, meditative atmosphere of a Taoist temple.) As a result, popular "religion" in China was happily syncretistic, and lacked any sophisticated overall "theology." There was no interest in, or quest for, revealed truth. While we might view the religious/theological scene as chaotic, to the Chinese the three forms of thought—in spite of their different emphases—were accepted as "three ways to one goal."

That goal was not a hoped-for eternal life, but rather a striving for the good life in this life. This humanism is the cultural/philosophical thread that has run continuously throughout Chinese history, even until today. The most articulate spokesman for Chinese humanism was the Middle Kingdom's greatest sage, Confucius.

A Scholar to Royalty

Confucius is the romanized name of K'ung Tzu, or Master K'ung. He was born in 551 B.C. in the Chinese state of Lu, in what is now the province of Shantung in eastern China. His ancestors had held positions of nobility in the state of Sung, but the family became embroiled in political troubles, and before the birth of their illustrious son had already lost its titles of nobility. This had driven them to migrate to Lu where Confucius was born.

Thus at birth he was a commoner and had to start working at an early age because of the family's worsening financial condition. By the time of his thirties, however, Confucius was a scholar whose reputation had already reached his ruler's ears. It seemed that his future was assured.

But all was not well in the state of Lu. China's great historian, Ssu-ma Ch'ien later wrote: "From the highest dignitaries down, every one was grasping power, and all had departed from the true way." Because of this turmoil, Confucius refused the offer of political office. Rather, he "lived in retirement, and arranged . . . the records, the rites and the music."

Not until he was fifty did Confucius choose to serve as a public official. The Duke of Lu appointed him as manager of a district, and it is recorded that within a year "his neighbors on all sides took him as a model." But Confucius carefully monitored the ruler's conduct and he did not like what he saw. Six years after accepting his post, he left government service because he saw how political intrigue had begun to erode the duke's ability to rule. The duke's political ineptitude was compounded by a not-so-modern flaw—wine and women.

Years of Wandering

For the next fourteen years, Confucius wandered from state to state in his never-ending attempt to teach his ideals of political and social reform. During this time he devoted his days to scholarship and teaching. It is reported that he gathered more than 3,000 disciples. While he taught, he also continued to try to influence the political leaders of the neighboring states, but with almost no success. He was convinced that the only way China could recapture its past greatness was to live out the moral law (the *Tao*, the way) as taught and practiced by the ancients. In that sense, Confucius was the untiring reformer, the pioneer. Further, he advocated universal education for all classes in Chinese society. No one, according to Confucius, was to be denied an opportunity to learn.

But on the other hand, Confucius—like most Chinese of influence throughout the nation's history—was also a prisoner of the past. Not a reluctant prisoner, to be sure, for he was a man who "believed in and loved the ancients."

He upheld the customs of the culture of the earlier Chou Dynasty of which reverence for heaven and a family's ancestors were an important part. Confucius maintained that "the superior man stands in awe of . . . the Mandate of Heaven." He taught that "if the way is to prevail, it is the Mandate of Heaven." And yet Confucius never failed to put the welfare of his fellow-men before those heavenly concerns.

When his disciples would ask Confucius about heaven and the life beyond, he was reluctant to discuss these "other world" phenomena. This silence led his students to say that the way of heaven "cannot be heard." When one disciple asked specifically about serving spiritual beings and about death, Confucius replied, "If we are not yet able to serve man, how can we serve spiritual beings? . . . If we do not yet know about life, how can we know about death?"

While Confucius valued the religious thought of earlier dynasties, when it came to contemporary practice, he chose not to make it an issue in his teaching. For Confucius, man and man alone was the measure of things. Heaven might have its peculiar influences on worldly affairs, but if the moral law—the *Tao*—were ever to be grasped, it would be because man himself grasped it.

His Program of Peace

Confucius lived during a time of tremendous political confusion. He was confident that his own program for stability and peace would bring the needed order and restraint to the people. Again, it was man—quite apart from celestial help—who would bring this about.

What has come to be called his "Peace Program" is perhaps one of the best examples of the humanism of the man. If man were not a sinner and was innately good, as Confucius believed, his plan could become a charter for peace. It breaks down, however, at the crucial point of man's nature which is incurably rebellious, lustful, violent and sinful. He cannot, within himself, do what Confucius expected him to do.

But here is the logical human reasoning of the ancient sage:

The ancients who wished to manifest their clear character to the world would first bring order to their states. Those who wished to bring order to their states would first regulate their families. Those who wished to regulate their families would first cultivate their personal lives. Those who wished to cultivate their personal lives would first rectify their minds. Those who wished to rectify their minds would first make their wills sincere. Those who wished to make their wills sincere would first extend their knowledge. The extension of knowledge consists in the investigation of things. When things are investigated, knowledge is extended; when knowledge is extended, the will becomes sincere; when the will becomes sincere, the mind is rectified; when the mind is rectified, the personal life is cultivated; when the personal life is cultivated, the family will be regulated; when the family is regulated, the state will be in order; and when the state is in order, there will be peace throughout the world.

The thinking expressed in that passage can best be summarized by the Chinese word, *jen* (pronounced *run*), which means simply "humanity." All Confucianist thought moves around this idea. Confucius defined "humanity" as "being respectful in private life, being serious in handling affairs, and being loyal in dealing with others."

Such a man was a "superior man," and Confucius believed every person alive had this innate potential. All he had to do was develop the qualities within his own spirit. This superior man, or "man of humanity," was one who "wishing to succeed, he also seeks to help others succeed. In a word, to be a man of humanity is to love all men."

In the turbulent China of Confucius' day, this was radical thinking. Few were willing to accept the challenge of Confucius to become this superior man, a fault that has lived with equal ease in a thousand other cultures since.

Preoccupied with the Practical

Humanism is at the base of all Confucius' educational, political and sociological doctrines. The sage argued that if you have good rulers, you will have good citizens. If people are guided by virtue, they will be virtuous. Without a good example, Confucius insisted, the people would run amok. He was simply stating what he had observed as being empirically true, and said it didn't have to stay that way. To his death, Confucius stayed preoccupied with the practical world. His message was simply that man was to do good. He didn't concern himself with the two larger questions dealt with by Jesus Christ: Why? And how?

Confucius insisted he was only a "transmitter, not an originator." He felt his obligation was to reflect the value of China's golden age—the ancient cultural heritage of sages of China's even more distant and glorious past. These values, he declared, would bring peace to the minds and hearts of Chinese who had long forgotten the importance of the moral law.

Seldom understood by the political power structure of the day, Confucius grew increasingly melancholy in his final years. He would heave sighs, and lament, "Alas, no one knows me."

He died at the age of seventy-three, and far from being unknown, his thought and teaching ultimately became the essence of what we know as China today.

Seeking the Stray Heart

The era following Confucius' death has been called the period of the "warring states" during which the political units of China fought for dominance. It was also an occasion for other numerous branches of philosophical thought to go into active competition with Confucianism. During this chaotic period of Chinese history, the teaching of Confucius declined.

The decline was to last for 100 years. That the teachings of the sage were restored to respect and acceptance at all, was due largely to Mencius (372-289 B.C.), a disciple of Confucius' grandson.

Confucius had held firmly to the doctrine of *jen*—"human-heartedness"—but he failed to explain why a person should act in this manner. Mencius tried to fill the gap, but he too was trapped in humanism, for he could only tell the people why. He could not show them how.

He, too, believed in the "original goodness of human nature," and his reasoning went this way: "All men have a mind which cannot bear to see the sufferings of others. . . . If now men suddenly see a child about to fall into a well, they will without exception experience a feeling of alarm and distress." His logical conclusion: "From this case we may perceive that he who lacks the feeling of commiseration is not a man."

Speaking in impassioned pleas, Mencius warned his society, " . . . if the way of Confucius is not seen, crooked words will bewitch people, and choke love and right. When love and right are choked, beasts are led to eat men, and men will eat each other."

He was sounding the alarm over a morally corrupt society. He narrowed his attacks to zero in on the leaders. "Sage kings cease to arise," he preached, "and the feudal lords give reign to their lusts. Unemployed scholars indulge in unreasonable discussions."

Strange as it may seem, one of Mencius' disagreements with other philosophical schools was that some were indiscriminate with their love—they loved *all* alike. Mencius taught benevolence, but he insisted that if love were to mean anything, it must be structured along certain levels—a liking for animals, a love for people, and deep devotion to kin. He taught: "A gentleman likes living things, but he does not love them. He loves the people, but not as he loves his kinsman. He is a kinsman to his kin, and loves the people. He loves the people and likes living things."

On the question of doing good, Mencius advised that it is man's duty whether or not it brings him profit. King Hui of Liang had asked the philosopher what gain his advice could bring to the royal house. Mencius answered sharply:

Why must you speak of gain, King? There is love, too, and right, and they are everything. When the king says, What gain can I get for my land? the great men say, What gain can I get for my house? the knights and common men say, What gain can I get for myself? then high and low fight one another for gain, and the kingdom is shaken. . . . When gain is put before right, only robbery can fill the maw. Love never forsakes kinsmen, right never puts his lord last. You, too, King, should speak of love and right and of nothing else; why must you speak of gain?

Whereas Confucius considered himself a transmitter of ancient thought, Mencius was a faithful interpreter of his master, Confucius. With appropriate humility he left this counsel, "The great man is he that does not lose his child's heart."

But perhaps his most significant statement expressed a spiritual longing: "If a man's dog or hen strays, he knows where to seek it; but when his heart strays, he knows not where to seek it."

Many Chinese philosophers were to look for that stray heart, but few would search with the innovative approach of the founder of Taoism.

The Way and the Power

Chinese scholar C.P. FitzGerald calls Taoism "the quietest philosophy of the profound minds." Traditionally, the ascent of Taoism in China is associated with the name Lao Tzu—the "old master." Lao Tzu was a teacher of the Way *(Tao)* and the Power *(Te)*. His doctrine taught the sublimation of self and emphasized the virtue of "namelessness." His was a mystical system of thought that seemed to speak of solid things without substance, of movement without moving. Lao Tzu said, "The *Tao* is eternal, nameless, the uncarved block. . . . Once the block is carved there are names. . . . The *Tao* is nameless."

One phrase that appears consistently in Lao Tzu's teaching is the Chinese expression *wu wei*—or "not to do anything for," generally translated as "inaction." But it is *active* inaction, an activity, according to Lao Tzu, that is more effective than either might or power. The phrase carries the idea of unassertive and quiet behavior which ultimately accomplishes more than pushy or aggressive behavior. Perhaps the best contemporary illustration of that philosophy in application is the passive resistance movement of American blacks in the sixties.

Lao Tzu is more difficult to understand than Confucius and it was reported that the two had strong disagreements. Confucius was direct and straight. Mencius underscored Confucius. Lao Tzu goes drifting off into the fog and says, "Come and find me." Yet it is in the Taoist scriptures—*Tao Te Ching*, which is the sum total of Lao Tzu's thoughts—that we get some of our most helpful clues in understanding the Chinese mind.

The *Tao Te Ching* gives a perfect application of the principle of *wu wei*, this silent, natural working of the *Tao*:

The highest good is like that of water. The goodness of water is that it benefits the ten thousand creatures; yet itself does not scramble, but is content with the places that all men disdain. It is this that makes water so near to the Way.

Nothing under heaven is softer or more yielding than water; but when it attacks things hard and resistant there is not one of them that can prevail. . . . That the yielding conquers the resistant and the soft conquers the hard is a fact known by all men, yet utilized by none.

Therefore the Sage
In order to be above the people
Must speak as though he were lower than the people.
In order to guide them
He must put himself behind them.
Only thus can the Sage be on top and the people not be crushed by his weight.
Only thus can he guide, and the people not be led into harm.

Indeed in this way everything under heaven will be glad to be pushed by him and will not find his guidance irksome. This he does by not striving; and because he does not strive, none can contend with him.

Lin Yutang, a sensitive interpreter of China to the West, calls Lao Tzu's work "the first enunciated philosophy of camouflage in the world." There is truth in Lin's statement. Lao Tzu is hard to pin down. He speaks of the wisdom of what seems to be foolish, the success of apparent failure, the strength of apparent weakness, the advantage of giving in, the futility of grasping for power.

It is not difficult to find teachings of Jesus which parallel these teachings exactly. Jesus' teachings on servanthood and humility are reflected in these words of Lao Tzu:

Only he that refuses to become foremost of all things
Is truly able to become chief of all Ministers.

There are more:

Never be the first in the world.
For love is victorious in attack and invulnerable in defense. Heaven arms with love those it would not see destroyed.
Requite hatred with virtue.
He gives to other people, and has greater abundance.

Dr. Lin tells his Western reader, "If one reads enough of this book [Tao Te Ching], one automatically acquires the habit and ways of the Chinese." If this is true, perhaps here is our key for understanding even the China of Mao Tse-tung and

Teng Hsiao-p'ing. A question we must continually ask ourselves is, "How much has China changed after all?" Lao Tzu wrote of the rhythm of life, the unity of existence, the importance of being simple, fear of too much government, the strength of active inactivity, the need for meditation and the weakness of force and assertion. Businessmen and politicians who deal with China today say that many of the cultural traits live deep in the Chinese they have met. Today's comrade in Peking may not call it the *Tao*, but his whole rhythm of life says he is still participating in it.

The Import from India

For nearly a thousand years Taoism overshadowed Confucianism in China. But the foreign doctrines of Buddhism attacked the sage's teachings even more fundamentally. The Buddhism which came from India in the third century B.C. brought new and fresh thoughts to Chinese minds that had been denied the luxury of diverse theological speculation. For the better part of a millenium it would be safe to say that the best thinkers in China were Buddhists. The Ch'an (Zen) school of Buddhism particularly, with its quiet meditative charm, flourished in Chinese minds.

The successes of Buddhism were due largely to the humanistic atmosphere that permeated China. While other-worldly in many aspects, Buddhism also adapted well to a man-centered environment.

As a result, Buddha was always understood by the Chinese in human terms. In what scholars feel was the first treatise on Buddhism in China, it was emphasized that Buddha was a *man* of moral achievements who "aimed at virtue." He was respected for his earthly goodness. Even the Chinese translation for the Buddha's name was *neng-jen*, translated as "the ability to be good." Many Chinese worshiped the Buddha as a deity. But the most popular form of the Buddha to this day is still the Kuanyin—a highly humanized figure of veneration and respect.

Throughout the years, Buddhism never lost its foreignness. And provocative and stimulating as the teachings of Buddha were, they went essentially against the grain of the traditional Chinese world view. Confucianists who sensed the threat of an expansive Buddhism also regarded the foreign teachings with suspicion. Loud outcries against Buddhism have gone up throughout Chinese history, and adherents of the Buddhist faith have always been prepared to endure their share of persecution, as they did during the mid-1960s Cultural Revolution.

That is the way it is with things foreign in China.

By the beginning of the Sung (960-1275) and Ming (1368-1644) dynasties, neo-Confucianism had succeeded in returning the Chinese mind to the old, established orthodoxy. The neo-Confucianists found it necessary to articulate their teachings with the

Buddhist threat uppermost in their minds. The import from India never disappeared, but it lost its impetus.

So the "three ways of thought"—Confucianism, Taoism and Buddhism—each left its mark on ancient China. And even though the relative popularity of each ebbed and flowed in succeeding periods of Chinese history, it was always Confucianism that emerged as the thinking of orthodox Chinese. This was largely because the ruling powers of China—themselves agnostic Confucianists—maintained an active distrust of the "cultish" popular religions that could so easily be turned to adverse political ends.

Religions that relied on the gods of the rivers, mountains and wind were difficult to control and often moved the populace to rebellion and unrest. So to be able to keep them under close scrutiny, it became an official tactic to patronize such movements as Buddhism and Taoism. Their shrines were cared for and their temples subsidized (an ancient Chinese method of maintaining control over splinter groups). If the emperor himself became too infatuated with something like Buddhism—as often happened—it was the duty of Confucian officials to bring him back to the orthodox Confucian way. While Taoism and Buddhism continued to gain converts, like Christianity, they never did make the inroads necessary to destroy the more deeply planted Confucian roots—also like Christianity.

Today and Tomorrow

The past is past, but what about today? Even more important, what about tomorrow?

How much of the spirit of Confucius still lives on in today's Chinese comrade? How much do the teachings of the Buddha continue to influence the Chinese peasant on his commune? Are there any Taoist "free spirits" left in China?

A few things can and should be said about Confucianism, first of all.

1. After a period of being put up as a national disgrace, Confucius is now being published once again. For the first time, some Chinese students actually hold his words in their hands. Others have been reading hidden copies of the sage all along in the privacy of their parents' homes.

2. At the same time that the ancient philosopher was being denounced, his teachings had so permeated the life of China that the government itself was taking on more and more the character of a Confucian family structure. As China scholar John Fairbank said in speaking of Mao: "The more he seeks to make China new, the more he seems to fall back on old Chinese ways of doing it." It is a fact that China is—and possibly always will be—a prisoner of her past.

3. Students escaping to Hong Kong have told interviewers that they never lost interest in China's past history and many were quietly instructed by

their parents. This was especially true as the Cultural Revolution began to wane and the youthful Red Guards felt disowned by Party leaders. The students were shattered. They had been told that old was bad, but now they found that "new" was ephemeral. Many turned to China's past to look for answers.

4. Many of Mao's thoughts printed in the "little red book" were couched in Confucian terms. Put those quotes in China's early history instead of the mid-1900s and they could have come from the mouth of the ancient sage himself.

5. Humanism is still the theme in China today. Everything will be done by man. Man is still the measure of all things. Confucius might not feel all that much out of place in the new China.

6. The family is still important—and still surviving—in spite of repeated attacks.

7. China still does not seem to express any desire to have a "revealed truth." Her centuries-old humanism set the country up for the dialectic of Marx and its emphasis on man alone.

8. We can only speculate that the thoughts of Confucius may once again be taught in Chinese schools. Perhaps not—at least, not as the orthodox way. But their simple entrance into Chinese minds will reactivate what is already latent there.

While Buddhism is still a foreign religion to China, it has survived thirty years of Communist persecution and propaganda, and reports indicate it is once again beginning to bud.

1. The government has given permission to print copies of the Buddhist scriptures which were long forbidden.

2. The Communist regime has paid for the renovation of a number of Buddhist temples and they have been reopened. Like Christian churches, most of them had been turned into warehouses, museums and grain storage depots.

3. Recently Japanese Buddhists met with their counterparts in China.

4. Joss sticks (incense) are in the public markets once again and are being used, especially in the villages. Undoubtedly, masses of people continued to use them all the time since the further away from Peking you lived, the safer it was to break the rules. However, it can be assumed that now many families are bringing their joss sticks out of the closet. The story is told that during the Cultural Revolution, a soldier came across an old peasant woman burning joss sticks in front of an ancestral tablet. The soldier asked why, and told her such activity was forbidden in the new China. The woman answered, "If you and the government can improve my lot, then I will no longer pray to the spirits."

Although it may be more difficult to specifically identify Taoist activities since it would be less structured than the other two, the ancient faith is certainly still prevalent in the country.

1. If Mao Tse-tung ran the country like a

Confucianist father would handle his family, he fought battles like a Taoist general, Sun Tzu, who lived in the sixth century B.C. In fact, Mao followed the tactics of Sun Tzu almost to the letter. Paraphrasing the old master, Mao said, "It is often possible by adopting all kinds of measures of deception to drive the enemy into the plight of making erroneous judgments and taking erroneous actions, thus depriving him of his superiority and initiative."

And Mao never bothered to point out the remarkable similarity of his sixteen-character jingle depicting his military strategy to several of Lao Tzu's verses:

1. When the enemy advances, we retreat!
2. When the enemy halts, we advance!
3. When the enemy seeks to avoid battle, we attack!
4. When the enemy retreats, we pursue!

The old master would have been proud of his modern disciple.

2. What the Westerner sees as inscrutability in the Chinese may simply be the spirit of Lao Tzu. There is still a strong feeling for the rhythm of life, the ebb and flow, the passive restraint.

Consider Chou En-lai's standard response to journalists when they would ask how long before Peking would take Taiwan or Hong Kong. He would say something like: Next year, or maybe the next, or fifty, or 100 years from now. Mao said virtually the same thing about the ultimate battle between socialism and capitalism.

The Way of *Tao* is not dead in China.

The People's Republic has declared that all religions are superstitious. Because Confucius had been elevated to virtual deity status, his philosophy fell under the same category. This message has come down especially hard on the ears of Chinese youths. All their lives, they have heard nothing but the Party line. All religion has been under attack, especially foreign religions. But now the foreigners are returning, even though in small numbers. This will give many Christians a chance to simply live their faith in a Chinese context. It will have its effect. It will change attitudes. It may be the vehicle for bringing people into the kingdom of God.

While Buddhism and the mystical elements of Taoism have been scorned, we know that necromancers still practice; fortunes are still told; joss is still burned, and people still pray for good luck.

With the waning of revolutionary fervor, a vacuum remains deeper than ever before. So these questions are pertinent:

If no Buddhism, what?

If no Taoism, what?

If no Maoist thought, what?

Students are going to ask about China's past, and

Confucius, Lao Tzu—and, perhaps, the Buddha—will again be subjects of intellectual conversation. Everyone wants to know more about his roots. The Chinese are no exception.

We can safely say that whereas Confucianism may never again be the ideology of the Chinese state, the spirit of the sage—the very essence of what is China—will continue to influence the Middle Kingdom for centuries to come.

A young Chinese raised on the *Four Books* is going to be different from one who has known only the thoughts of Chairman Mao and the Party propaganda handouts. The ink on those political tracts will fade, but the never-to-be-erased thoughts of Confucius and the sages of ancient China will remain. China has always respected the past. This will not change.

And in the process of this new discovery, new philosophers will emerge in China. Perhaps there will be another Lao Tzu. Why not another free-spirited, anti-establishment person who will lead his own group of liberated thinkers to that other drumbeat?

Even if it sounds like double-talk, it's still true: In China, everything has changed and nothing has changed.

That truth will help us more, perhaps, than anything else to respond appropriately to what we see happening in China today.

Wall Comes Tumbling Down: Chinese tourists and soldiers at a section of the Great Wall of China at Badaling.

Peking University: Bicycles are a status symbol for students and for others.

UPI 5-10-67

A cathedral used as a food storehouse, towers high above the rooftops of the city of Canton.

New highrise apartments in Peking. Construction has been accelerated to provide improved housing conditions for city residents.

Peking residents reading wall posters proclaiming resumption of diplomatic relations between China and the United States.

The Stars and Stripes at full mast above the U.S. Liaison Office in Peking. A Chinese military guard keeps watch.

UPI 1-5-79

6
God Was in China Before Marx

You will receive power when the Holy Spirit comes upon you; and you will bear witness for me . . . to the ends of the earth.

Jesus Christ

More than 400 years before Marco Polo blazed the trail of commerce to the Far East, the riches of Asia had already attracted other traders from the West. Taking the land route from the Middle East, a seventh-century version of a modern "trade delegation" arrived in the Middle Kingdom. It most certainly was not the first. The one which appeared in 636 A.D. is generally believed to have come from Syria and was headed by a man named Alopen.

In addition to being merchants and traders, the group was also devoutly Christian.

How much of the motivation for such an arduous journey was pure commerce and how much was missionary zeal, we do not know. Probably it was the latter cloaked in the former. We do know that

Emperor T'ai Tsung welcomed them with open arms.

The Nestorians Arrive

Alopen himself may have been a monk. Some think so. We know that some of his party were members of religious orders. They were from the Nestorian movement, a Middle Eastern expression of the Christian faith which emphasized simple worship, use of the Scriptures and missionary outreach.

The emperor, representing the benevolent and tolerant T'ang dynasty, gave them full access to the royal court. A follower of Confucius, T'ai Tsung was much distressed over the spreading influence of Buddhism, and may have seen in the new faith a counterbalance to the imported doctrines from India. He invited Alopen to a one-on-one audience at which time the Christian was asked to expound his faith to the emperor.

It must have gone well because the emperor permitted the Christian books which Alopen had with him to be translated and three years later he ordered that a church and monastary be built in the capital city of Ch'ang An.

T'ai Tsung also issued a proclamation. It said:

The Way has more than one name. There is more than one Sage. Doctrines vary in different lands, their benefits reach all mankind. O Lo

Pen, a man of great virtue, has brought his images and books from Ta T'sin. After examining his doctrines we find them profound and pacific. After studying his principles we find that they stress what is good and important. His teaching is not diffuse and his reasoning is sound. This religion does good to all men. Let it be preached freely in our Empire.

But the emperor did not personally embrace the Way. Perhaps the proclamation was an early application of a slogan heard in the land today: "Make foreign things serve China." That slogan, revised and cast in new words, may be the key to understanding everything that has happened—and is happening—in China.

The story of the introduction of Christianity into China is known because in 1625 a nine-foot monument was excavated in a village not far from the ancient capital and it contained a rather full account in both the Chinese and Syriac languages. A cross is carved into the top of the huge tablet and the opening phrase has been translated: "A monument to the diffusion through the Middle Kingdom of the brilliant teaching of Ta Ch'in" or more popularly stated, "The introduction and propagation of the noble law of Ta T'sin in the Middle Kingdom."

Historian Kenneth Scott Latourette says that Ta T'sin or Ta Ch'in was the Chinese name for the Middle East.

So the Christian faith had an early and auspicious beginning in China. But it was not to last—and that has been the historical pattern. The Nestorians enjoyed moderate success for about two centuries.

However, with the ascension of Emperor Wu Tsung, a follower of the indigenous Tao religion, Christianity received a severe setback. By imperial edict, both Buddhist monks and Christians were outlawed. The foreigners were expelled. Yet evidence indicates that a century later some modest degree of Christian activity remained. But within two centuries, the story was different. One ancient Syrian writer tells of meeting in 987 A.D. a Nestorian monk who, with five colleagues, had been sent to China seven years earlier in an attempt to pull things together and save the vanishing church. He reported, however, that the faith had disappeared in China and that he had been able to find only one Christian.

The Quiet Centuries

That may have been too pessimistic a report. However, as far as the church in China is concerned, the next 600 years could be called "the quiet centuries." Politically, the area was in ferment. Genghis Khan led his Mongol hordes out of their ancestral lands in the heart of Asia and gained control of China. While the Mongols themselves were primarily animistic, like the Chinese emperors before them, they also found religion to be a convenient political tool. In an informal *quid pro quo* with China's new masters, the Nestorians began to gradually rebuild.

In the latter part of the thirteenth century, Marco Polo found evidences of Nestorian Christianity in many parts of China.

Roman Catholicism, having by then established itself in most of Europe, began to look toward Asia. In 1294, the first Catholic missionary, John of Montecorvino, arrived at the court of the Khan.

But neither Nestorian nor Catholic Christianity put down any indigenous roots in Chinese soil and that represented an important failure. The Mongol rulers responded no more to Christianity than did the earlier Chinese emperors. The western Mongols embraced Islam and those in the south held to Buddhism.

And while this was happening in the further reaches of the empire, the Nestorians and Catholics engaged in shameful rivalry around the capital of Khan-baliq itself. This infighting was about the only activity among Christians to disturb those quiescent centuries. They stole each other's converts, fought for the favor of the royal court and in general discredited their own testimony.

As the church in China was growing weaker, Tamerlane arose to become the terror of the western wing of the empire. The first of his clan to embrace Islam, he conquered and slaughtered with a religious fervor. The Chinese used this diversion in the west to overthrow the Mongol dynasty and once again become masters in their own land.

And they wanted a land without the gospel, which they still viewed as an alien religion. And they were not far from right. Although there certainly were some true believers among the Chinese people, the leadership of the churches remained foreign even after centuries. Little or nothing had been done to make the church "Chinese," either in leadership or in culture.

This was not the only failure. With typical Western superiority, the early missionaries made no attempt to understand Chinese culture and customs, assuming they must be inferior and even incompatible with the Christian faith. Western forms of worship were imposed with no regard for what might be inappropriate. The Nestorians apparently learned very little Chinese, while the Catholics stuck with Latin and even instructed their converts in that ancient language. Finally, there was the bitter, self-destructive rivalry between the two groups.

It would seem that those early efforts to establish the gospel in China were not so much destroyed by the Chinese as they were sabotaged by the Christians themselves.

The Jesuit Thrust

Two centuries were to pass before another major attempt was launched to plant the Christian flag in

China. Europe was suddenly exploding all over the world—and every time a new land was "discovered," it was claimed in the name of God and of the ruler of the explorer's country, all in the same breath. It was the era when Columbus happened into America and Magellan proved the earth was not flat.

Following the trail that had been blazed by Portuguese traders, members of the Jesuit order made their way to Cathay in the mid-1500s. The Mongols were gone and the Middle Kingdom was back in the hands of Chinese rulers. In fact, it was the time of the brilliant Ming Dynasty. Tamerlane's death had spared the country a bloody war with Islam. China would have been quite content to settle down once again in splendid isolation.

But Europe's desire for China's riches and the church's commitment to Christianize all pagan lands made that impossible. The missionary fervor of the Society of Jesus, founded in the 1540s by Ignatius of Loyola put that group in the vanguard. The first Jesuit to appear on Chinese soil was Francis Xavier who landed on a small island in the south. Although Xavier died from fever before he could penetrate the mainland, others were challenged by his vision.

The most notable was a priest with "curly beard, blue eyes and a voice like a great bell" named Matteo Ricci who landed at Macao in 1582. A culturally sensitive man, he set out to understand China before he attempted to evangelize it. He decided his first efforts should be made in the direction of the scholars who were highly influential. If they could be persuaded to believe, others would follow. Ricci's own scholarly credentials—geography, mathematics and astronomy—gained him a hearing from these mandarins and he received from his own superiors permission for his fellow priests and himself to wear the robes of scholars.

He was not without mistakes, but he knew how to recover and to adapt. The story of his maps provides a classic example. When he unrolled them for inspection by the Chinese intellectuals, the atmosphere suddenly turned frigid. Ricci had put Europe in the middle. It may have been all right to show America flanking Europe on the left, but Asia on the right? An insult!

Father Trigault who translated Ricci's journals makes a telling comment on the episode. The Chinese were quite sure that:

> the heavens are round but the earth is flat and square, and they firmly believe that their empire is right in the middle of it. They do not like the idea of our geographies pushing their China into one corner of the Orient. They could not comprehend the demonstrations proving that the earth is a globe, made up of land and water, and that a globe of its very nature has neither beginning or end. The geographer was therefore obliged to change his design and . . .

he left a margin on either side of the map, making the Kingdom of China to appear right in the center. This was more in keeping with their ideas and it gave them a great deal of pleasure and satisfaction.

Together with his map-making ability, Ricci brought with him European inventions, including clocks, a quadrant and a clavichord. George Patterson says in *Christianity in Communist China* that Ricci's method " . . . became the standard of both Roman Catholics and Protestants in later centuries—Christianity was identified with learning, techniques and material benefits of the West."

Ricci sought to find ways to make Christianity more palatable to the Chinese intellectuals, his target group. Some would call him a compromiser; others would say he was adopting Saint Paul's strategy of becoming all things to all men. At any rate, he managed to strike an accommodation with prevailing Confucianist philosophy by declaring it to be a system of ethics rather than a religion. He didn't attack ancestor worship directly, but sought to give it a less heretical meaning under the cloak of filial piety. Whenever possible, he used Chinese religious terminology to describe unique Christian doctrines. For example, he adopted the Chinese expression, *Shang-Ti*, as his word for God. The Chinese used it to describe in a vague sense the highest Being.

All this brought Ricci and the Jesuits into sharp conflict with the newly-arrived Franciscans and Dominicans who were already in the streets with their crosses and European garb, creating quite a furor among the populace. They simply could not comprehend any Christian doctrines being expressed in any form other than those in traditional usage in Europe.

News of the sharp conflict reached the emperor (the Manchus now ruled the land), who was furious that foreigners should presume to decide things regarding the Chinese. A decree was issued: "Henceforth no European missionary will be permitted to spread his religion in China. Thus we shall avoid further trouble."

Amazingly, the Christians once again had succeeded in doing themselves in.

The Protestant Turn

For about two centuries there was no foreign missionary activity in China. Not until the nineteenth century did Protestants develop a missionary vision, but when they found it they mobilized quickly.

By 1850, missionaries representing the London Missionary Society, the Baptists, the American Board (composed largely of Congregationalists), the Presbyterians, the Methodists and the Anglicans were serving in China.

They, too, came on trails blazed by traders—and

by soldiers. It happened this way. The British especially wanted to expand their trade with China, but the Chinese still feared foreign influence on their culture and wanted the trade to be a one-way street flowing outward with tea, silk and curios. As far as imports were concerned, the emperor told King George III, "We possess all things."

Actually, there was one thing they didn't possess—opium—and the British decided to use that as the means of balancing their trade deficit. It doesn't make very nice reading in the annals of a so-called "Christian" nation, but history is history. Acquiring opium in Southeast Asia in return for Western manufactured goods, the merchants—primarily British—sold it in China, thus creating an ever-expanding market for the addictive drug. The emperor banned by imperial decree what was called "foreign mud," but the foreigners were not accustomed to allowing the Chinese to order their own trade affairs. The attitude was: Who are these Chinese to be telling us what they should import?

That clash of interests brought about the Opium Wars (two of them) with Great Britain. The Chinese lost both. In the imposed settlements, the British got Hong Kong, a number of port cities were opened to foreign trade and residence, full diplomatic recognition was given to the foreign powers and foreigners were permitted to travel freely throughout the country.

In return, the Chinese got missionaries—for the

final part of the treaties provided that missionaries were free to teach and preach anywhere in the empire and Chinese were guaranteed the right to become Christians.

Churches in the West viewed this as being an answer to prayer and the sovereign intervention of God on their behalf. Undoubtedly, the Chinese took a less enthusiastic view. It is important to understand this if we are to correctly understand what happened to Christian missions in China in the twentieth century.

In his splendid work, *The Church in China*, William H. Clark comments: "The 19th century brought pressure unparalleled, humiliation and agony such as China had never experienced in its 4,000 years of recorded history. The despised and feared foreigners, those hairy, high-nosed, seemingly uncivilized barbarians, actually seized much Chinese territory, dominated her economy, threatened her very existence and civilization as nothing had ever done."

It is generally conceded there was not a single Protestant Christian to be found in China on January 1, 1800. In 1853 there were 350 communicant members. By 1889, there were 37,289.

And it all started with a man named Robert Morrison. He arrived at Canton in 1807, the first missionary of the London Missionary Society. Morrison had to go to New York and book passage on an American ship, however, because the British

East India Company which controlled shipping to China wouldn't sell him a berth. They were concerned that an idealistic young missionary just might impede some of their immoral trading activities.

In the course of the long voyage from New York, the American captain asked Morrison if he really expected to make an impact on China. He replied: "No, sir, but I expect God will."

Morrison became a serious student of the Chinese language and made a monumental contribution to missions both then and later by translating the Bible as well as other important literature into Chinese. He died in his early fifties and, like Xavier before him, was buried in Asia. At the time of his death he could number only ten converts, but it would be a mistake to try to measure his contribution in terms of numbers.

As the Protestant missionary movement gained momentum, others followed. In the first half of the nineteenth century, American missionaries outnumbered the British by about two to one even though the total number of sixty-eight was still relatively small. The popularity of Americans at this time was due largely to the fact that the United States had opposed the opium traffic and the Chinese considered them better qualified than the English when it came to expounding on moral law.

But a new impetus was given to Protestant missions just after 1850 with the arrival in China of

James Hudson Taylor. Although Taylor came under the Chinese Evangelization Society, he later founded the China Inland Mission and issued a call for 1,000 missionaries. There were nearly that many in his society alone when he died in 1905.

The land to which they came was in deep trouble. There were rebellions and uprisings. Warlords ruled and peasants submitted. Social justice was unknown, as were human rights. Corruption and gambling were rampant. Opium undermined health and morality. Famine and epidemics ravaged the country.

During the great famine of 1877-79, one missionary wrote in his diary:

> Heard stories at the inn that night of parents exchanging their children as they could not eat their own, that one dared not go to the pits for coal as mules, donkeys and their owners were liable to be killed and eaten . . . I heard from other eyewitnesses that they had seen 270 dead on the roadside in three days . . . small wonder that I began to doubt my senses or my sanity, amid such scenes of horror. Was I among the living or the tormented dead?

The Christian gospel spoke not only to the need for personal salvation, but also to the desperate human need. Hospitals and schools were built in large numbers and Latourette describes in one of his volumes the additional issues to which the missionaries addressed themselves: "They fought the age-old custom of binding the feet of women, combatted the production, sale and use of opium . . . sought to ameliorate the lot of the blind, the deaf, and the dumb." Orphanages were founded and urgent appeals were made to the churches back home for famine relief.

A great deal of good was done, but the Chinese could never forget that those who came to them in the compassionate name of Jesus Christ, came on "missionary gunboats" with the backing of Western powers who exploited their country's weaknesses every chance they got.

Persecution Strikes

Although the missionaries did not take part in the injustices forced on China by the Western powers, they did take advantage of every political and military victory to push the gospel further into the mainstream of Chinese life. As a result, the Chinese found it impossible to distinguish Christian motivation from the rapacious ambitions of the foreign political powers. This was to have serious repercussions in the twentieth century.

There seemed to be no end to the humiliations forced on China. After her defeat by Japan in 1895, the Western powers moved in to divide up the spoils. Germany took over a large section of Shantung province, Russia demanded free use of two Manchurian ports, and the British pushed through a ninety-five-year lease on the Kowloon Peninsula just across from Hong Kong. France insisted on a similar lease to territory in Kwangtung.

These were only a few of the concessions demanded and received as the Western powers put their heel on China's neck. But inevitably a reaction set in against anything foreign—and Christianity was included.

History calls it the Boxer Uprising and it bore the unofficial stamp of approval of the Empress Dowager. At the heart of it were the local militia units, but they gathered around them ragtag elements not noted for their gentility. Their name was given to them by the foreigners who observed that the various gymnastic exercises they performed made them look like boxers.

The trigger for the uprising was an order—either genuine or forged—from the empress, Tz'u Hsi, calling on this rabble to exterminate the foreigners in the land.

The foreign enclaves in the major cities became armed fortresses and church compounds were turned into fortified camps. But missionaries who were scattered throughout the interior without the protection of an enclave or a compound were the most vulnerable and suffered the heaviest losses. When the uprising was put down a year later for foreign military intervention, it was found that 188 Protestant missionaries and their families had been murdered along with forty-four Roman Catholics.

If there could be any good news out of so much bad it would have to be that the martyrdom of thousands of Chinese Christians at the same time proved that finally the gospel was putting down roots in the alien soil of China.

Latourette estimates that 30,000 Chinese Catholics died for their faith during the uprising and that there were 2,000 Chinese Protestant martyrs. For the first time in nearly 1,300 years, the Chinese church was showing a spiritual vitality that encouraged optimism about its future.

Twenty-five Years of Growth

The first twenty-five years of the twentieth century was a period of unprecedented growth of the church in China. Missions flourished. The Boxer Uprising had forced many missionaries into temporary exile, reducing their numbers to about 1,000. But by the time of World War I, that number had multiplied to 5,000.

During that period there also occurred what J. Edwin Orr calls "the Chinese quickening." This revival, which was felt in all parts of the country, came in three phases, according to Dr. Orr: "There was a prayer movement between 1900 and 1905; there was a widespread awakening in 1906 and 1907; and there was extraordinary revival throughout 1908 and 1909, continuing until the revolution in 1911."

An interesting sidelight to this revival is the fact

that it spread among Chinese university students who were studying in Japan. Many had gone there after the Russo-Japanese War—including a young man named Chiang Kai-shek—to acquire Western ideas. A church was formed in Tokyo to shepherd the 250 students who became followers of Jesus Christ.

On the mainland, even the staid denominations were experiencing the emotional impact as God's Spirit moved to convict and convert thousands. Sins were publicly confessed, simultaneous prayer broke out among hundreds with no confusion, and attendance in the churches swelled. Among those used by God in the awakening was a Presbyterian missionary from Canada, Jonathan Goforth. In describing what happened, his wife wrote:

> Again and again during these days when dozens were praying at once and when everyone seemed to be weeping, there came a wonderful sense of quiet. For at such times no one spoke or prayed or cried aloud. The presence of God never seemed more real.

A British missionary sensed a breakthrough:

> We know now that Chinese are emotionally susceptible in matters of religion; we know now that 'instantaneous conversion' may be seen in China as in Chicago or London. We know that

the longing for the fulness of the Spirit, with accompanying willingness to sacrifice all for its attainment, may be felt in Shensi as in Keswick.

Perhaps the most significant result of the revival movement was the surfacing of national Chinese evangelists. They were mightily used by the Spirit and it seemed as if, finally, the Chinese church was coming into its own.

While the Catholics were growing rapidly (nearly two million members in 1918), the Protestants began to move in two divergent streams. One was pietistic and highly evangelistic while the other was oriented toward the meeting of social and human needs. This was to have a profound effect on the coming revolution, for many of those in the latter group were to welcome the socialist goals of the Communist Party.

The Communists Emerge

The years between World War I and World War II were generally quiet years for the church in China. Growth continued. National leadership increased in numbers and matured in strength. But politically, the stage was being set for dramatic confrontation, conflict and change. The republic founded by Sun Yat-sen in 1912 was in difficulty because of his inability to deal decisively with the warlords who still controlled much of the country.

Having been denied assistance by the United

States and Great Britain in getting rid of his internal enemies, Dr. Sun turned to Russia for advice and help. This move gave status and legitimacy to the newly-formed Chinese Communist Party and led to an alliance between the Nationalists and the Communists.

Enter Mao Tse-tung, one of the Party's founders.

In the meantime, the young student who had been in Tokyo returned home to China. He was recruited by Dr. Sun for leadership in the Nationalist Party (Kuomintang) and later married the sister of his mentor's wife, the lovely and talented Soong Mei-ling.

Enter Chiang Kai-shek who, incidentally, converted to the faith of his wife, the daughter of a Shanghai pastor.

So the stage is set for conflict. A bitter struggle soon developed between the two former allies which was an off-again, on-again affair until after the Japanese were defeated in World War II. At that time the struggle blew up into open battle and the alliance was off forever.

The missionaries had generally supported the Nationalists because the Communists had early demonstrated their hostility to Christians by driving them from the areas they controlled. It was actually a choice between the lesser of two evils, for the Nationalists were not without their faults. There was much corruption and inequity under Chiang Kai-shek's government. But in all fairness, it is a gross misrepresentation to paint the Nationalists as black as the Communists—or blacker, as some have done. With all his faults, the generalissimo governed better than anyone who had preceded him. There was freedom, albeit somewhat limited, and Chiang himself was an honest man.

His fault—or at least one of them—was his loyalty to friends who were dishonest. But who would deny that his government was infinitely better than that which followed?

If the missionaries had committed themselves politically, many of the national Christian leaders waited to let the political dust settle. And when it settled in 1949, Chiang Kai-shek was on Formosa with tens of thousands of his closest followers.

And Mao Tse-tung was in Peking.

The church in China was entering a new era.

7
Truth on
the Scaffold

Truth forever on the scaffold, Wrong forever
on the throne—
Yet that scaffold sways the future, and, behind
the dim unknown,
Standeth God within the shadow, keeping
watch above his own.

James Russell Lowell, in *The Present Crisis*

Father John Tung knew the crisis was at hand.
He could delay no longer.

Inexorably, the screw was being tightened. Just as
the people were leaving after Mass that Sunday, a
carefully timed Communist demonstration passed
by the church. The congregation of Catholic faithful
were forced to join the marchers as they shouted
slogans against the papal representative in China:
"Down with the imperialist Riberi! Let the
government expel him!"

Now it was late afternoon in Chungking and a final
massive demonstration was supposed to conclude
with denunciations of the Internuncio before the
huge crowd. The regime was trying to build public
support for its campaign to have Monsignor Riberi

labeled a "lackey of the imperialists" and to thumb a collective nose at Rome.

Father Tung made an unscheduled appearance at the microphone. It was the moment of his personal crisis and he knew what he must do. First, he traced on himself the sign of the cross and then he began to speak, using words familiar to every Catholic, for it is the way every sermon begins: "In the name of the Father and of the Son and of the Holy Ghost."

A hush fell over the demonstrators. It was as still as inside a cathedral when the forty-five-year-old priest continued.

"The point of what I wish to say is this: I offer myself as a sacrificial victim to bring about an understanding between the government and the Church. . . .

"It is those very people, who deny the existence of God and of the immortal soul, who do not recognize the Vicar of Jesus Christ on earth—the Holy Father—and the position of the hierarchy in relation to the Catholic Church, who would claim that the 'three independencies' [self-government, self-support, self-propagation] program is merely a patriotic movement.

"They profess the freedom of religion and admit the spiritual ties between believers and their religious superiors, but by this same 'independence' I am today required to attack the representative of the Holy Father. Tomorrow I shall perhaps be forced to attack the representative of Jesus Christ, the Holy Father. The following day why should I not then be constrained to attack God Himself? . . ."

A murmur went through the mob. Father Tung pressed on:

"Since the government has time and again insisted that they are not forcing us, but simply directing us, then I ought only to speak from my heart, and not have said 'yes' with my life, and 'no' in my heart. I ought only to sign those declarations to which I sincerely consent and not affix my name to those with which I disagree. If I live by deceit and fear death, I become a completely untrustworthy man, of use to no one. . . ."

His voice now was firm with conviction:

"I make these statements now being of a sane mind and I avow that whatever I may say later in a state of confusion will be entirely invalid. I am a Catholic and desire to love both my country and my religion. I do not wish discord between the two, but if the government cannot work harmoniously with religion, persecution will follow and many victims will be demanded from among Catholics. In such an event it is better that I die right now!"

The priest stepped down and the demonstration ended in total confusion. The Communists did not know how to deal with one brave man, but they soon recovered and in less than two weeks Father Tung was arrested—and he simply disappeared.

As hundreds of thousands of Christians were denounced, arrested, imprisoned and executed, the church found itself with many heroes and heroines. Sometimes they were in the ranks of the laity. When 4,000 Catholics were brought together to witness the mock trial of the Bishop of Shanghai, not a single one would denounce him. Instead, each time his accusers tried to humiliate him, the people would cry out, "Long live our bishop!"

The Saga of Wang Ming-tao

Protestants had their stalwarts as well and preeminent among them was a highly popular lay preacher from Peking named Wang Ming-tao. He fearlessly wrote and preached against both the Communists and fellow Christian leaders whom he felt had compromised themselves by collaborating with the regime. Both felt the sting of his words, but they dared not touch him because of his popularity with the people.

Finally, in 1954 they moved against him. An accusation meeting was called at which the fundamentalist pastor was accused of (1) lack of sympathy for the government, (2) refusal to participate in the Three-Self Movement (discussed later in this chapter), and (3) "individualistic" preaching with an unclear purpose.

Throughout the entire meeting he never once stopped looking up and he never spoke a word. When the demand for his death was put to the crowd, only about one-fourth voted for it, so his persecutors could take no action. He resumed preaching to larger crowds than before. Hundreds stood in the cold outside his church and listened to his sermons over loudspeakers. It was obvious that the government would have to deal with such a troublemaker.

Before daylight on August 8, 1955, he and his wife were awakened and taken off to jail with eighteen student members of his congregation. He was sentenced without trial to fifteen years in prison. His crime? Having "no feeling for the people, for he has a heart of lead."

He was released after thirteen months, but during that time he had been completely broken by two Communist agents who were placed in his cell with the order to "reform his thoughts." His health was ruined and he was no longer able to work. But more tragically, his mind and spirit had been broken. The regime called a meeting to "welcome" his release at which time he was called on to read a paper he had written. He confessed that he was a "counter-revolutionary offender" and said he was guilty of "sabotaging various government plans and the Socialist reconstruction movement."

This man who preached one of his last sermons against collaboration on the subject, "Betraying the Son of Man with a Kiss" had written the following after his brainwashing:

As a result of the patient attitude shown by the Government and the reeducation given me, I have come to realize my errors. I have been accorded generous treatment by the Government and have been saved from the abyss of crime. For this my heart is full of gratitude.

Reports from people who saw him said he was filled with remorse and deep depression, alternately accusing himself of being Judas and Peter. Later both he and his wife repudiated his so-called "confession."

That brought immediate retaliation in the form of house arrest. Before long, however, he was returned to prison. Unsubstantiated reports received in Hong Kong indicate that he died in the early 1970s.

Making Peace with Caesar

But not all the church leaders resisted the regime. Some were simply tired of fighting and believed anything was better than the constant civil war. Others believed the friendly initial Communist overtures and decided to make their peace with Caesar. Still others enthusiastically identified themselves with the Communist goals.

The first couple of years of Communist rule were fairly benign. No overt action was taken against the churches. In fact, Chou En-lai met with a group of Protestant leaders in Peking in 1950 and after assuring them that he thought Christianity was a superstition, he said: " . . . we are going to let you go on teaching, go on trying to convert the people; provided you also continue with your social services. After all, we both believe that truth will prevail; we think your beliefs are untrue and false, therefore if we are right, the people will reject them, and your church will decay. If you are right, then the people will believe you; but as we are sure that you are wrong, we are prepared for that risk."

But the smooth words were not matched with honest deeds. Instead, one year later, 151 Protestant leaders were brought to Peking to start the Three-Self Reform Movement. Most of them participated wholeheartedly. The "Three Selfs" meant that the churches were to be self-governing, self-supporting and self-propagating. Those were worthwhile goals which the missions themselves had desired, but the Communists twisted them into an "anti-imperialistic" stance which made them highly political and supportive of the regime's objectives.

Y. T. Wu, secretary of the YMCA, was at the front of the movement, fully cooperating with the government. He wrote:

It is due solely to the Chinese Communist Party that the Chinese people today can stand erect, receive these blessings and have such a bright outlook for the future. . . . If the "miracles" that Christianity believes in are true, then the fact that the Chinese Communist Party in the short space of thirty years has enabled the Chinese people, exploited and oppressed for thousands of years, to stand upon their feet, and at the same time enabled the Christian Church to throw off the shackles of imperialism, is a miracle of a sort heretofore unheard of.

It was Wu and the other leaders of the Three-Self Movement who set out to change the mind of Wang Ming-tao and win him over to their side. When they failed in their mission, they were the ones who denounced him. It was toward them that the lay preacher directed his most powerful sermons and they had to silence him.

The Communists used a similar strategy to deal with Catholics. A "patriotic" church was established with no ties to Rome and bishops, priests and people were invited to join the puppet organization. Most refused and intense persecution fell on the church.

Professor Arthur Glasser of Fuller Theological Seminary, a missionary in China during the Communist takeover, states that "by 1948 one could draw a straight line across China in almost any direction and find functioning churches every twenty to thirty miles." When the Communists came to power in 1949, it is estimated there were three million Catholics and 800,000 members of Protestant churches. The total Christian community probably numbered over five million.

What remained of the visible church after 1949,

both Catholic and Protestant, soon disappeared because its spiritual integrity had been betrayed by compromise.

The real church went underground.

Did Missions Fail?

Some would view this removal from the scene of all institutional forms of Christianity a massive failure for missions after several centuries in China.

But this is not necessarily so. That is not to say that missions could not have done better. Almost anyone can have twenty-twenty hindsight. Nonetheless, missionary efforts in China did have some serious weaknesses. Almost as soon as the missionaries were ousted in the early 1950s, a post-mortem of the mission effort was begun. Professor Glasser identifies at least eight mistakes:

1. Abysmal ignorance of Chinese history and culture. Most missionaries were convinced that everything Western was superior to anything Chinese and saw no reason to absorb what to them was an obviously inferior culture. Frequently they regarded the Chinese with "irritation, condescension and contempt."

Sadly, this attitude on the part of Americans and Europeans still exists all over the world today and I have seen it in some of its most obnoxious forms. How can we ever truly love and respect a people if we have no appreciation for their past?

2. Careless indifference to local customs. This

attitude alienated the missionaries from both the ruling class and the common people. The gentry found them insensitive to long-standing customs and judgmental about anything which offended their Western sensibilities, even though no moral issue was involved. The common people resented them because of their readiness to identify China's endemic dirt, suffering and disease with moral corruption.

3. Aggressive proclamation of Western values. The West was held up as the example of what China should become. Christianizing was generally equated with Westernizing. This was usually accompanied by a tragic unawareness of the effect these abrupt efforts to displace Chinese standards would have on the social and political fabric of the nation. How often has the identification of the gospel with Western cultural values been a handicap in the presentation of a message which is universal!

4. Public denunciation of idolatry. Obviously, they were on solid biblical ground in doing this, but the Chinese didn't understand their motivation. They interpreted this as political subversion because it challenged the semi-divinity of the emperors and undermined the Confucian system of public order.

5. Rejection of ancestor worship. Again, this was perfectly understandable and justified from their Western and Christian frame of reference. It was unquestionably against God and the Bible. Unfortunately, the Chinese knew very little about

either and they viewed this stance as a condemnation of all forms of filial piety.

6. Opposition to local religion. So much of the cultural life of the villages was tied into ancient religious beliefs that the missionaries forbade their converts to participate in all religious festivals and theatricals. This was regarded as an attack upon the communal structure of rural China. As with most of the other shortcomings, a little understanding and patience in this matter might have gained for the missionaries an open ear instead of a closed mind.

7. Careless use of the Scriptures. Because some portions of the Old Testament described the actions of people in a different time, place and culture, it seems they should not have been given to the people without adequate explanation and teaching. (The British Foreign Office specifically cautioned missionaries regarding their use of Joshua, Judges, Ruth and the Song of Solomon.) The distribution of these Scripture portions without helpful commentaries confused the Chinese and led them to believe that the Bible was diametrically opposed to the public order.

8. Establishment of extensive compounds. Under the "foreign rights" which had been forced upon China following military victories, missionaries acquired land and then put up impressive buildings for homes, school and chapel. Some of the churches were even of Gothic design which could not have appeared more out of place in

the midst of traditional Chinese architecture. The compounds containing these buildings were walled-in and declared free from government intervention by virtue of the missionary's nationality.

This "foreignness" became even more galling as the missionaries interceded to protect their converts from lawsuits and provided for their social needs in times of disaster while excluding the nonbelievers from assistance. The missionaries and their compounds were regarded as the beginnings of "foreign enclaves, set up to take over the country."

It is not necessary to deprecate the devotion and sacrifice of those missionaries in order to see their weaknesses. A more important question than "Did missions fail?" is "Did we learn anything from these mistakes?" There is no clear evidence that we have learned very much—and that may be a greater tragedy for missions than getting thrown out of China. George Santayana was right when he said: "Those who cannot remember the past are condemned to repeat it."

How Fares the True Church?

When the Communists subverted and successfully destroyed institutional religion in China, they eliminated the organizational forms of some 150 denominations and missions which had come from the West.

When that happened, it was both interesting and

sad to see how quickly China went out of Western church thinking and the missionary vocabulary. It had once occupied such a large place in prayer, concern and giving. How short was the Christian memory! When the missionaries left it was almost as if the Western world thought that God, too, had been evicted from China.

There was much moaning over China's "closed door," a syndrome with which I've never had much sympathy. Closed to whom? Certainly not to God. He is not limited to our understanding of open doors and He doesn't require a visa to gain entry. In fact, God never left China.

He stayed with His church.

But hardly anyone from outside ever sees the church in China today because it is dispersed, decimated and deep underground. Father James B. Wang, a priest who is also a professor at the University of Montana, went back to China in 1977 for a visit. Writing in *Christianity Today*, he describes what he saw: "The China I remember was dotted with temples, pagodas and churches with a constant flow of worshipers through their doors. Yet . . . I saw no open churches or temples. Religion is not taught in schools and religious books are not sold in the bookstores. No one discusses religion, either publicly or privately.

"I looked for Catholic churches. I found civic centers, social institutions, schools and stores. I saw fallen or tilted crosses on rooftops and wondered whether the younger generation knows what they mean. I walked through my old high school grounds; the school was founded by the Marianist brothers. We rode by my former seminary with its beautiful Gothic cathedral. The buildings are almost intact—just as I remember them. But the atmosphere is different."

Protestants see the same thing on guided tours. In Peking they may attend a church service where they will see some diplomats and tourists, but only a handful of Chinese worshipers. This and two Catholic churches are the only open churches in the capital city of ten million people.

Yet it would be wrong to say that this is the total picture of Christian life in China today. A senior China watcher says, "There are two Chinas: the mythological China and the real." Perhaps. Or maybe there are many Chinas—or a single China of many hues. Whichever it is, conditions vary so greatly that almost anything you would say about the church in China is true somewhere in the vast country.

David Adeney, a former missionary to China, calls it "an uneven picture" and divides the land as follows: (1) areas where Christians are isolated, (2) areas where Christians enjoy fellowship and (3) areas of revival.

Certainly believers have a tough time of it in most of China. A medical student tells of studying in a town where there were a number of Christian families, but they found it impossible to worship together. The home in which he stayed was that of a Christian professor whose wife would gather the family for secret worship. After carefully closing the doors and windows, they would sing a hymn and then read the Scriptures and pray. They used a Bible which the student had brought with him. It had been preserved from the Red Guards by his grandmother who wrapped it in old cloths and buried it in a flowerpot.

Adeney says he talked to one young man who came to Hong Kong with his five-year-old daughter to visit his father. He had left his wife behind in an area where Christians feared to speak their faith. He said that sometimes he and his wife prayed together in bed but they had not told their little girl about Jesus because they were afraid she would mention the name in kindergarten and bring trouble to them. She heard the stories about Jesus for the first time in Hong Kong.

A very different picture is given by a young woman who now lives in Hong Kong but goes back to her village for occasional visits. Hers is a peasant family and all the members are Christians. She says that some of the local cadres are also Christians.

She describes worship this way: "We meet regularly in people's homes. We observe Saturday as the Sabbath and normally do not work that day. People attend various house meetings whenever they are free and interested. Usually there is a meeting in someone's home every night."

Some members have been assigned the job of visiting other house churches in the area and shepherding members and recent converts. They are paid a regular amount from the offerings received.

This church, an indigenous group which never had foreign connections, is growing. "Only recently about 100 people in our area were baptized," she reports. "It was during the winter and one local cadre jokingly told us we should not baptize so many small children and elderly people. They might catch cold and have to report to 'sick bay' the next day. The cadre said if that happened, he might get into trouble with his boss. Fortunately, nothing happened and no one caught cold."

Some areas have reported the outbreak of revival. In one place there were between 4,000 and 5,000 baptisms in 1976. These were conducted mainly at night or in some remote spot. According to an eyewitness, a carload of soldiers was sent to interrupt one of these baptismal services which was being held up in the hills. Their jeep broke down and before they could get it repaired, the meeting had ended and the Christians had scattered to their work in the fields.

In this same area, mass meetings would sometimes be held in an out-of-the-way place with as many as 1,000 attending. One such meeting lasted several hours "with teaching, singing, testimonies and a great sense of the presence of God in their midst." As the meeting ended, five young men stood up and said they had been sent to make arrests, but they had been so impressed with what they had seen and heard that they, too, wanted to believe.

Many of the stories have the ring of primitive, simple New Testament Christianity. One official arrested some Christians and was questioning them about what they did. Among other things, they said they prayed for the sick and told him of those with apparently incurable diseases, including cancer, who had been healed. The official told them that he himself had cancer and asked if they would pray for him. As a result, not only was he healed, but he also came to faith in Christ even though it meant suffering, for he himself was later arrested.

Christian Life in a Village

A friend of mine, Dr. Jonathan Chao, dean of the China Graduate School of Theology in Hong Kong, conducted a most interesting interview with a young lady who had left China. She grew up in a village in Chekiang province, went through school, and participated in the Red Guard movement during the Great Cultural Revolution. But through her grandmother and frequent letters from her parents who had emigrated to the United States, she became a Christian.

In her village there were about 300 families, of whom six were Christians. In another village of about 100 families, less than four miles away, about 30 percent were Christians. One production brigade in that village, numbering between twenty and thirty families, was entirely Christian except for one family.

Portions of the interview will give some intriguing insights into evangelism in at least one village.

Q. How did it happen that an entire production brigade turned Christian?

A. In that particular production brigade there were two or three families who were unusually zealous for the Lord. They were really willing to pour themselves wholly into prayer for the salvation of the entire production brigade. They helped everyone who needed their help. Non-Christians in that village were exceedingly moved. They felt it was great to be Christians. So they, too, believed in the Lord. Another important reason is that wherever Christians are active, the devil is also extremely active. At one time there were many in that village who were possessed by demons. Not a few were mentally sick, too. So all the Christians prayed for them and they were healed and the demons were expelled.

There is real power in the prayers of Christians. When they pray for the demon-possessed, demons flee away. But if a person does not confess his sins thoroughly, the demon returns to him and he becomes re-possessed. But if his whole family prays sincerely and wholeheartedly, and the demon-possessed person himself confesses his sins thoroughly and then the Christians pray for him, the devil will flee away, never to return to him again.

Q. If a person gets sick and the Christians pray for him, will he be healed?

A. Yes, usually, except sometimes in cases of prolonged chronic illnesses. But demon-possessed persons are usually healed at once after prayer. Demons flee away as soon as Christians pray. This is really marvelous. You may not believe this, but I have seen demons expelled.

Q. Now that the sick are healed and demons are exorcised by prayer, what kind of impact do these events have upon the non-Christian community?

A. They feel it is great to be Christians. But Christians have no status in China. When national movements are staged by the Communist Party, Christians have to eat "the bitter and the sour." They undergo persecution and suffering. So many do not want to become Christians themselves, but they highly respect those who are. Only those who are utterly helpless—those who have no way out—come to Christians for prayer.

Q. In addition to healing and demon-exorcising by prayer, what are some other factors which lead the people to believe in the Lord?

A. One other important factor is that parents are

usually able to, and eventually do, lead their children to Christ, or at least one or two of them. This personal approach extends to relatives and friends, too.

Q. Do Christians in your village and those in the other villages meet together for worship and fellowship?

A. Yes, they meet on the Lord's day. Until 1962 we had a church in our village. But after the Cultural Revolution (1966-69), all services were terminated. During that period Christians could not have fellowship with each other. If they congregated for fellowship, they would be called in by the battalion headquarters for interrogation. Christian leaders or preachers would be put under "struggle." They would be placed on an accusation platform built in the center of the village, and everyone would come and "struggle" against them. But after the first high wave of the Cultural Revolution had passed, Christians resumed personal fellowship, and restored their night meetings or met together during rainy days.

Q. So rainy days are meeting days!

A. Yes, and so are evenings. Usually those of us who lived near each other got together. Someone would get the word around and we all would gather together. Often there were no preachers . . . but many elders from the pre-revolution days now assume the responsibility of preaching.

Q. Did you have Bibles in your village?

A. Yes. The Bibles we used were almost entirely preserved in the homes of those who belong to the category of "lower-middle-class farmers." For example, my family was designated as "nondesirables" because my father used to work with the former Nationalist government. Therefore, we could not keep Bibles. During the Cultural Revolution the Red Guards entered homes of our category and searched everywhere, so it was impossible to have a single Bible preserved.

Q. Who are the nondesirables?

A. They are seven classes of people known as the "seven black kinds": landlords, capitalists, rich farmers, rightists, anti-revolutionary elements, capitalist roaders in positions of power, and "no-goods."

Q. Are they regarded as noncitizens?

A. They cannot enjoy the privileges of citizens. Their children are called "children of the seven nondesirables."

Q. Tell us about the pastor's daughter who went about preaching.

A. She used to live in a town about thirty-five miles away from us. She had a junior high education which is considered pretty good by us villagers. Her father used to be a pastor and she also has the gift of preaching. She really preaches very well so we often asked her to come preach to us. She was also frequently invited to preach in Shanghai, being escorted there secretly, of course. She has been invited to preach in most of the counties in our province. But she still has her own work. If one does not have a regular job, he or she is suspected by local authorities.

Q. Do Communist cadres know about your Christian meetings?

A. Sometimes they do. In our neighboring village, the mother of the secretary of the production battalion became a Christian so there was nothing he could do. His mother was once very sick. She sought help from doctors everywhere, but she could not get help. So as a final resort she asked friends to invite Christians to come to her home and pray for her. The Christians really prayed for her time and again for two months and finally she was healed. That is when she became an earnest believer. So then the Christians went to the cadre's home for meetings.

Q. During periods of national movements, were Christians affected?

A. Yes, but the lay people were usually left alone. Preachers sometimes got into trouble during those periods. But if you were a lower-middle-class farmer and you went around preaching, nothing serious would be done to you even if you were caught. You would be lectured, of course. But if you were one of the seven nondesirables, then you could expect trouble.

The Church Lives On

It should surprise no one that the church in China is still alive. Jesus promised that "the gates of hell shall not prevail against it." It may lack many of the supporting comforts which we in the West consider necessary, but it undoubtedly possesses a vitality and strength unknown to her contemporary counterparts in much of the rest of the world.

David Adeney says it grows primarily "through the personal life style and behavior" of the people of God. He tells of a friend who was staying in a hotel in a Chinese city. His friend was much impressed by the attitude of a woman who was sweeping the floors. One day he was able to get her alone and he asked if she was a Christian.

She replied that she was, adding, "I cannot say much about my faith, but I seek to show my love to others; and sometimes when people ask me, I can talk about the Lord Jesus."

Dr. Chao provides this magnificent summary:

"The secularized church in China has become religionless, and yet she possesses vital religion. Stripped of her former denominational fragmentism, she has come to sense a new dimension of spiritual solidarity. She has lost her clergy, but has become a kingdom of priests. No longer able to enjoy her Gothic churches, she yet experiences the reality of body life. Without missions, she yet has become missionary herself; appearing to be impoverished, she is exceedingly rich; seemingly weak, she has survived persecution; no longer hearing sermons, she practices them daily.

"The resultant Christianity in China is a church that has been thoroughly purged by red fire. Such a church is, no doubt, very precious to her Lord. She is a cleansed and sanctified vessel of honor prepared for every good work."

8
Out of the Trial by Fire

"Truth, crushed to earth, shall rise again;
The eternal years of God are hers.
William Cullen Bryant

Crowds gathered around the wooden bench as a recent visitor to China sat down to rest. They were intrigued by this foreigner who could speak Chinese.

"Where did you learn our language?" they wanted to know.

He told them he had once lived in China.

"And what did you do here?" they asked.

He told them he had been teaching in connection with the Christian church. He said he recognized the importance of material things, but that he was convinced man also had spiritual needs which could only be satisfied through faith in God. He spoke about the large number of Christian students in Hong Kong.

A young man responded: "I agree that faith is useful, but only a few old people here still believe. Young people do not have the opportunity to study religion, but they are free to believe if they want to."

Soon the dialogue was finished and the crowd began to drift away. One young man stayed. When all the rest were gone, he began to speak: "What the man in the crowd has just said is not true—there is no freedom." He poured out his own deep feelings of dissatisfaction. He was not a Christian, but he had a hunger for spiritual things. He came from a Christian home, but during the Cultural Revolution his home had been sacked and the Bible burned.

Before the visitor left, the young man had committed his life to Jesus Christ.

While that story tells the experience of only one young man, I believe it speaks volumes about the ideological and spiritual vacuum which exists in China today.

A Vacuum through Violence

When the Communists took China in 1948, they became masters in a land where traditions and beliefs went back over many centuries. Confucianism and its accompanying ancestor worship had its roots so deep in Chinese life, culture and religion that it seems it would have been impossible to have produced a national "conversion" in the short span of twenty-five years. But Mao and his band of followers came out of the caves of Yenan determined to achieve nothing less than that.

In order to establish the beliefs of Karl Marx and create a new social order it would be necessary to destroy the old order and especially the religious elements in it. That meant not only Christianity must go, but the ancient religions as well. The revolution must be total in order to produce a totally new man for the classless society. Whatever would challenge Marxist ideology had to be eliminated.

The Communist cadres set about their task with a stout, and often bloody, determination. They found that some of the institutional forms of Christianity could be made to serve socialist ends. These organizations were enfolded into the Marxist system and craftily subverted until they were made over into the Communist image. The pastors, priests and teachers in these organizations were frequently recruited as participants in the virulent campaign against "unfriendly" religious elements. They were paraded before populace and foreigners as the occasion demanded to parrot socialist slogans in support of the regime.

It is true, however, that most of these collaborators genuinely believed in the rightness of what they were doing. The evils and inequities of the previous systems, they felt, made the professed equality of socialism a highly desirable goal to be attained. This was the position taken from the beginning by one evangelical leader, Marcus Cheng. His words shocked his colleagues: "Only the doctrines of Marx and Lenin give the science of revolution and the instrument which will set society free. . . . From the heart I can sincerely say that I fervently love Communism and accept the teaching of the Communist Party and the teaching of Mao Tse-tung."

The president of a Christian women's college also enthusiastically supported the Communist cause and justified her position as follows: ". . . as a patriot, I must do all I can for a regime that has ended corruption, inflation and starvation and has already brought us for the first time in a century a generation of peace. . . . Finally, and you may find this hard to swallow, I support the regime as a Christian."

But huge numbers could not be convinced and those who could not be subverted were systematically discredited and/or destroyed. God alone knows the number of martyrs who chose to die rather than deny their faith.

Christianity was not the only faith deemed alien by the Communist regime. The ancient religions were also suspect because in Marx's view all religions "are the opiate of the people."

This included Buddhism. During the Cultural Revolution, a Japanese journalist visited a photographic exhibition in Peking. What he saw was meant to show the anemia of traditional religions when contrasted with the red-blooded devotees of social change.

One picture shows an old woman destroying a statue of a bodhisattva [statue of Buddha]. The caption explained that when an earthquake occurred it was not the Buddhist saint but Mao Tse-tung who helped her. The next picture showed her destroying the old charm to give place to a portrait of Mao Tse-tung, and a new portrait of smiling Mao in military uniform was hung in the old family Buddhist shrine.

Buddhist temples were turned into granaries and warehouses. When a visitor asked what happened to the Buddhist monks he was told, "They have been secularized," which translated means, "They are cultivating rice and carrying night soil like all good citizens in a classless society should do."

The worship of ancestors, a cornerstone of Confucian religion, was also forbidden and the old sage was portrayed as an elitist reactionary who was against the people and whose bland teachings ("At home be humble; at work be respectful; with others be loyal") were meant to keep the rich and privileged in power and the peasants in subservience.

Thus with one stroke the new powers in China intended to remove all traces of religion, both ancient and recent, from the cultural scene. Their purpose was to establish more than a new political system—they intended to form a new man in a new society. Mao was the living revelation of 'god,' who was the people, and the socialist state was going to be heaven-on-earth.

When James Reston, a senior editor of *The New York Times*, saw this grand experiment aimed at remaking the Chinese people, he said he was amazed by "the staggering thing that modern China is trying to do. They're not trying merely to revolutionize people, and establish a sense of social conscience, but they're really trying to change the character of these people. The place is one vast school of moral philosophy."

Where the Experiment Failed

After thirty years of social experimentation has China succeeded in creating a "new man"? Has the new order arrived?

The answer is no.

It is one thing to destroy what a people have believed. It is quite another thing to replace that with a convincing and satisfying ideology. When someone mentioned that it was easy to found a new religion, Napoleon is supposed to have answered: "Of course. All one has to do is get himself crucified and rise again the third day."

By cutting the cultural and societal roots of China's present generation, Mao had succeeded only in leaving a gaping emptiness. His miscalculation was in believing that man, who is innately and incurably religious, could be fulfilled in a materialistic society provided you could keep the revolutionary fires burning in his heart.

He forgot that "every man is born with a God-shaped vacuum which only God can fill." There is strong evidence that such a vacuum exists in China today. The present state of the Chinese mind should not have been hard to predict. Forecasting required only the most rudimentary knowledge of human nature. After creating a spiritual vacuum by destroying the old value system and the cultural patterns of centuries, Mao tried to fill it with himself. He was the "brightest red sun" in the hearts of the people. "Mao thought" became the basis of doing everything from raising children to casting pig iron in backyard furnaces. When a team of Chinese young people won the world Ping-Pong championship, they were described as "bubbling with revolutionary zeal . . . particularly after studying and creatively applying Mao Tse-tung's thinking."

If you wanted to live to a ripe old age, you had to play ideological make-believe. People learned to mouth the slogans, but the words began to sound like rote instead of conviction. The masses thought it in their best personal interest to keep up the charade. Nobody wanted to be the first one to reveal that—in the words of Hans Christian Andersen—the emperor had no clothes.

And then the "great helmsman" died. Suddenly, it was as if you had pulled the ideological rug from under millions who had cut their teeth on his "little red book." Mao, too, was a man and his feet were clay. Gradually a few people began to say they had known all along that the whole thing was a game. Mao had been wrong, they said. Some even said he was all bad. Seeing that the criticism would get out of hand if the lid came off, Teng Hsiao-p'ing felt it necessary to state publicly that while Mao may not have been 100 percent good, he was certainly not more than 20 percent bad and he could still be trusted.

The critics got the signal and toned down their words, but the poster campaign continues. Cracks are beginning to show in the closed society and I doubt that it will be possible to completely seal them ever again.

Filling the Vacuum

The first law of physics is that nature abhors a vacuum. You prove that law every time you open a can of vacuum-packed coffee. Even before you smell the aroma of roasted coffee, you hear that sound of air rushing to fill the vacuum the moment you break the seal. That "whoosh" is simply Mother Nature being herself.

I believe there is a spiritual law comparable to the scientific law. Man was not made to live in a spiritual void. He needs to believe. It is essential to his emotional and social well-being. Someone has said, "A man can put up with any 'how' if he has a 'why.'" It is the "why" that drives him to God. Nothing else has ever worked as a permanent substitute—not materialism nor human ideology. The absolute need for God is described in the Bible in these picturesque words: "As a deer longs for a stream of cool water, so I long for you, God. I thirst for you, the living God" (Ps. 42:1, TEV).

Having produced the vacuum in China by destroying all religions, Mao was never able to fill the need for a transcendental faith with socialist humanism. If you believe in a sovereign God who is in control of history and who is able to make men's wrath praise Him, then you must believe that the events of the past thirty years have been woven into the strategy and plan of God for China.

Without for a moment endorsing the system or approving its bloody and brutal oppression of the Chinese people, I firmly believe that Communism has been an instrument in the hand of God to help prepare the country for a mighty invasion of His Spirit. The Holy Spirit is just waiting for the right moment to rush into those hearts which have been turned into vacuum spaces by the misguided zeal of Mao and his revolutionary cadres.

The return to religion in China is now so open that it cannot be kept a secret, although it is not necessarily Christianity to which the people turn. They are looking for anything which will speak to the needs of the heart. Fortune tellers, once very big in daily Chinese life, are now practicing openly again. Taoist priests are being called on to perform religious rites at family functions.

Time magazine says: " . . . many practices of the feudal past are observed. In the privacy of their own homes, there are many peasant families who still pray to Kuanyin, the goddess of mercy, and burn incense to their ancestors."

Incense is back on the market to meet the demand and *Time* goes on to report that "in the supposedly sophisticated cities, people often visit abandoned temples to pray for the success of some endeavor" (Jan. 1, 1979).

Among those most susceptible to the Christian witness, according to reports, are the young people. Having grown up in a religionless environment, they have no emotional ties to the ancient faiths. They simply want reality and it is reported they are seeking out practicing Christians in whom they notice a difference and are asking questions like "What makes you different?"; "How can you be happy all the time?"; "What gives you peace of mind in the midst of so much difficulty?" and "How can I find what you have found?"

A Christian doctor discovered that the manner in which he practiced his profession was his best witness. People took special notice of the kindness he showed to those who were labeled by the government as "nondesirables." It is estimated that at least 5 percent of the population have been so designated and they are discriminated against in many different ways. Any act of kindness shown them is certain to make a strong impression.

A young man whom I shall call Ching escaped to Hong Kong some time ago. He told an interviewer of the emptiness of his life under Communism and his insatiable hunger for meaning and reality. Ching was only a toddler when his Christian father escaped to Hong Kong. He and his brothers were left behind in the care of their mother who understood little of Christianity. But she had enough simple faith to teach her boys to bow in thanksgiving before meals. Then Ching learned in school that this "God talk" was merely superstition.

When Ching was about ten years old his mother was taken away by soldiers to stand trial in a public accusation meeting. The children were terrified. Ching threw himself on his bed and cried, "God, if you are real, please show me that you are the true God by bringing mama back." Before the night ended, she came home. Her name had been last on the trial agenda and the time ran out before the authorities got to her.

Ching began his spiritual search then, but it was not until he was nearing the age of twenty that he found peace. He had his father's Bible and a copy of a devotional classic, *Streams in the Desert*, and Ching recalls, "I had a deep inner need and hunger to read and pray every day."

He finished his education and taught for one year, but the emptiness persisted so he quit his job and turned totally to his search for meaning in life.

Determined to read his father's Bible completely through, Ching isolated himself for two months, straining his eyes hour after hour beside a flickering oil lamp. By the time he came to Romans 5, the full meaning of sin and redemption gripped his heart.

His search was over.

Because China is so huge and there are no channels of Christian communications within the country, we are able to put together only scattered pieces of a giant puzzle. But the evidence is clear. There is great spiritual hunger throughout China and God has not left himself without witnesses to step into this vacuum.

Jonathan Chao's description seems accurate: "Christians in China are not going out of their way to convert others, but nonbelievers, seeing something desirable in their lives, want Jesus for themselves."

Is the Attitude Relaxing?

A magazine published in the West headlined a story late in 1978 this way: "Christianity on the Way Back." That is certainly too optimistic a statement for the moment, but there are notable signs that the official attitude toward religion may be relaxing in the People's Republic.

The new constitution adopted in March, 1978 gave at least lip service to religious tolerance. It even created a Ministry for Minority Religions and a member of the Peking People's Revolutionary Council was appointed as the first minister. On paper, the constitution guarantees freedom to worship or not worship and to propagate atheism. Maintenance of old churches and temples becomes the responsibility of the state and monks and ministers become entitled to a monthly allowance and medical allowance from the government.

Even if all this could be taken at face value—and there have been no reports of celebrations in China—it would have little if any effect on the house churches and nonstructured form of the body of Christ active and alive in China today.

However, it is significant that references to religion in the Chinese press increased considerably in 1978. This included descriptions of temples and shrines as well as such varied articles as one on the discovery of the Dead Sea scrolls, participation by "religious believers" in protests in South Korea (the first such mention) and the visit of President Tolbert of Liberia, a Baptist clergyman, with Chinese Protestant leaders. In addition, an official release told of the completion of minor repairs on some fifth-century Buddhist temples.

By far the most dramatic reporting, according to Paul Kauffman of *Asian Report*, appeared in The *People's Daily* published in Peking. It was the impressions of a Chinese journalist about religion in American life. He reported that "Christianity occupied a dominant place in the United States." The journalist, Wang Joshui, observed that religion was obviously not a "crime" and not an "opiate of the people." It is, he said, simply a necessity of daily life. Most amazing of all, he included this sentence, quoting the French philosopher, "As Voltaire said, if God did not exist, it would be necessary to invent him."

But that was not the end. Wang also related what could have been his first encounter with the Bible: "There was a Bible in every hotel room. When we visited the White House, we saw two books on the desk of the American president—one was a Bible. The Bible is America's best-selling book," he wrote, "selling about 8.5 million copies a year."

What is the Church Like?

The church that exists in China today would not fit the typical Western understanding of what the church is. We think of buildings, programs, institutions and the like.

The church in China is probably best described in noninstitutional terms. It is the body of Christ, a fellowship of believers, a community.

David Adeney gives seven characteristics which mark the church in China and suggests that churches elsewhere might study these qualities in preparation for the day when Christians in other parts of the world will themselves pass through the fires of tribulation.

1. It has been purified by suffering. There are no ulterior motives for people joining the church. A woman from Hong Kong, who had been through

great difficulties in China because of her faith, said, "In China if a person joins us, we have a real Christian; but in Hong Kong we are not so sure."

2. Love and loyalty to Jesus Christ is central in the thinking of the Chinese Christians. They realize that a commitment to Christ involves obedience and taking up the cross.

3. The power of prayer has become very real to them. They experience the healing ministry of the Holy Spirit and see other people delivered from disease and demonic oppression in answer to prayer.

4. Loyalty to one another is essential. They have learned to uphold one another in times of difficulty and realize the importance of mutual trust, for if one betrays the group, great suffering follows.

5. It is a church rooted in the home and integrated into the family system and so finds itself free from the Western trappings of the past. Foreign buildings are no longer used and the organizations and types of meetings so familiar to Christians in the West do not apply to the church in China.

6. It is a church which witnesses more by actions than by words. There is little opportunity for preaching to nonbelievers. The Christians show their faith by lowly acts of service and love to their neighbors.

7. The Word of God is precious. Although they lack teaching and do not have the Scriptures readily available, they show their love for the Bible by the way they copy and share portions of it.

Thus the church in China may be closer to true New Testament Christianity than any other body of believers in this century. It not only survives, but grows, in spite of its difficulties.

Jonathan Chao has another salutary word in this regard: "It seems to me that the Spirit of the Lord is doing great works among the Christians within China, many of which are simply unknown to us. Perhaps it is not even necessary for us to know, lest we abuse that knowledge to their harm.

". . . God in His incomprehensible way, and even by the hands of the atheistic Communists, has liberated the Chinese Church from her former weights of Western traditionalism, divisive dogmas, hardened structures and fragmented denominationalism. Stripped of these external weights she has learned to look only to Jesus, and patiently run her heavenly race in this world as good citizens of the People's Republic of China. As an institutionless community of the redeemed, she has become a sign of hope to those in despair. Seemingly restricted, she probably enjoys more spiritual freedom than most of us care to admit."

When Will the Door Open?

The new day in China generates considerable enthusiasm and expectation among those who hope for a return of Western missions. We still think of "open doors" as meaning full access to China by missionaries. In 1971, shortly after China extended a tentative feeler to the West by an exchange of table tennis teams with the U.S.A., I received in the mail an announcement of a program designed to evangelize mainland China.

The letter asked: "Will you be one of the preachers and captain one of the 1,000 three-man teams for an evangelistic crusade in one of the 1,000 cities of China?" I was exhorted to help America "be first with the message of Christ as this great nation opens its doors to the outside world again!"

The communication came from a very responsible person, but the presumption of the plan appalled me and reminded me of a question asked by a sensitive Asian Christian: "Does God always have to come through New York?"

Perhaps some words of caution are in order here for those who, seeing the bamboo curtain opening a crack, would rush to kick it down instead of waiting for God's timing.

First, almost nothing has changed in China and it is naive to read the crack in the curtain as being anything more than that. Whatever contact the Communist regime allows with the Western world will serve their purposes, not ours. They are asking for technology, not theology. They want a few specialists and technicians, not preachers and missionaries. Their objective is to bring China up to the rest of the developed world in scientific achievement, not re-create Western ecclesiastical structures. To read anything more than that into the Great Leap Outward is merely wishful thinking.

Second (and paradoxically), almost everything has changed in China. There is little indication that we really understand this. The West does not really know the new China. Time did not stop when the Communists came to power. The social and cultural landscape has been radically altered. Unless we find out how and to what extent China has changed, we will waste valuable time preparing to evangelize the China of 1948 which no longer exists. We must do our homework. Only a concentration on data gathering, research, analysis and prayerful planning can save us from the folly of ill-conceived programs founded in ignorance which waste our three most precious resources—time, money and manpower.

Third, before we take even one step we must demonstrate an understanding of the sensitivity and restraint which are reflected in the Asian character. Many of our gentle friends from that part of the world are offended and frightened by our bulldozer, megaton approach to everything. A refugee said after some months in Hong Kong, "The churches here are so program oriented that I can't find any spiritual help for me as a person. On the mainland, when one Christian does find another, we try to minister to each other."

When I heard those words, I thought, "Who wants to instruct whom? There is so much we in the West need to learn."

Before the prophet Ezekiel spoke a word, he sat for a week and felt the heartbeat of a captive people.

If God were to widen the crack in the curtain enough to allow any of us to go through, we would find an incredibly pure church, refined in the flames of suffering. It might be more appropriate to respectfully ask to sit at their feet than to stand in their pulpits.

Fourth, when China is evangelized it will almost certainly be by Chinese and Asians. Why is that we always have this obsession to send Americans to do God's work in the world when the same amount of money will send three or four non-Westerners who do not look like colonialists? Every missionary agency needs to answer that question.

Do we have the humility and courage to ask the churches in Asia, "May we be your partners in evangelizing by helping provide some of the money and perhaps some personnel?" This internationalizing of missions, stripped of Western Christian imperialism, would be a magnificent demonstration of the validity of our message in the nonwhite world.

I have never doubted that God could save China from Communism. I just hope that when He does, He can also save her from well-meaning but heavy-handed American evangelical opportunities.

The Chinese in Diaspora

Of the 962 million Chinese in the world—almost one-fourth of the world's population—42 million of them live outside the mainland. They are called the

Chinese in *diaspora*—the scattered people. They are found in every country.

While the cell groups of Christians within China today must certainly be regarded as the primary source of future evangelistic activity on the mainland, the Chinese in dispersion must also be considered a potent factor in any evangelistic strategy.

Although only 5 percent of them are Christians, the church among overseas Chinese is growing and maturing. It is also possessed with an expanding missionary vision. A recent survey revealed nearly twenty-five Christian missionary agencies among them with evangelistic activities in as many countries.

Moses Chow, a missionary leader among Chinese in the U.S.A., speaks optimistically about the evangelistic potential of his people. As a race, he says, they have been adventuresome and pioneering, immigrating against great odds and risking their lives for the unknown.

He writes in the *Logos Journal*: "They are adaptable in business, language learning, adjusting to new places, people and climates. They are mobile, not needing any 'base' for support.

"Their color is neutral in this world of conflicts over extremes. Their endurance is proven; they have survived against great hardships and obstacles. They have a cultural background of creativity, initiative and inventiveness; their heritage of philosophy and deeper thought equips them to deal with the nations. They tend to be prosperous as a result of industriousness and perseverance.

"If these natural resources can be under God's control by the Holy Spirit," he concludes, "the millions of Chinese in *diaspora* will not only be evangelized but thrust into the mainstream of God's plan for His church worldwide."

Jonathan Chao shares that view, but tempers his optimism slightly with three conditions. He says: "The potential of Chinese churches for future missionary outreach among our own people and to the world at large is extremely great if (1) Chinese church leaders learn to love each other more and trust the young; (2) the gulf between evangelicals and ecumenicals can be bridged without diluting the core content of the gospel and discipleship; and (3) foreign missions and churches provide the needed encouragement, support and cooperation in mission tasks among the Chinese."

There is encouraging evidence that the Chinese church in *diaspora* is rising to the challenge. Large numbers of students on campuses in Hong Kong and Taiwan are being reached for Christ. The 7,000 Chinese nurses in London are a target group for the Chinese Overseas Christian Mission which has a person working full-time among them. In the U.S.A. there are over 250 Chinese congregations plus many more Bible study groups and mission agencies whose aim is to reach the half-million

Chinese in North America.

In Hong Kong some Chinese Christians became burdened for a small town in northern Thailand which is called the "South Gate to China" because it is so near the border. Just across the border from Maesai is the mountain village of Mang Fang which is packed with refugees from Yunnan province. Several of the Hong Kong Christians went to Maesai determined to find a way to get the gospel into China literally through the back door.

After several frustrating attempts to gain a foothold, they finally had a breakthrough when several Chinese from Mang Fang accepted Christ at one of the evangelistic camps held by the Hong Kong Christians. Since the border in this area is quite porous, they invited the lay evangelists to accompany them back to Mang Fang and start a church.

Two other groups of believers were established in nearby villages. The "missionaries" went on evangelistic tours in the mountain areas and attracted great crowds through the use of gospel dramas. There have been baptisms among people who previously were not only unreached, but generally considered unreachable.

Now additional teachers have been recruited to join the pioneer team. The effort is an outstanding example of how the Holy Spirit is using the Chinese in *diaspora* and indigenous methods to break into impenetrable areas.

By faith it is possible to see a great multitude of people coming to Christ from the Middle Kingdom. God has been preparing the country and the church for such a glorious moment. It will come as surely as truth, crushed to earth, does rise again. For Jesus promised, "Upon this rock I will build my church; and the gates of hell shall not prevail against it" (Matt. 16:18).

The church in China will come up out of her trial by fire some day, purified and triumphant, to the praise and glory of Jesus Christ, her Lord.

9
China Is More Than Chow Mein

Since it is not granted us to live long, let us transmit to posterity some memorial that we have at least lived.

Pliny the Younger

The Chinese merchant sat down at his cluttered desk in the back of the little store. It looked like scores of other little shops along the main street of Dungan, a small town on the east coast of Malaysia. I had stopped there to buy some food and supplies for a boatload of Vietnamese refugees who had arrived the night before. Finally, the list was complete.

The shopkeeper rustled around under the papers on his desk and pulled out one of those marvelous Japanese exports, a pocket calculator. I watched the diodes emitting red lights come alive as he turned on the switch. His fingers started to move over the keyboard as he tallied up my bill. He made a mistake, cleared the keyboard and started again. Once more the stubby fingers made a mistake. This time he turned off the switch, pushed the modern device away with a grunt and picked up a much used, very worn abacus.

After a few seconds of clacking the beads on the *suan pan*, or counting board, he announced the total of my bill with a smile of satisfaction. The tried and proven had triumphed. All that could be said for the new was that it was new, not necessarily better.

The same point might be made of quite a few things which have been China's contribution to civilization. Because Western history is so much tied to Europe and its achievements, the Chinese people have been cheated out of credit for more than one invention. Which reminds me of a comment made by one of my American Indian friends regarding the claim that Christopher Columbus discovered America. "My people knew it was here all the time," he said.

Take printing, for example. The Chinese were using movable type 400 years before the German printer, Johannes Gutenberg, "invented" it. True, Gutenberg may have known nothing about the achievement of a printer named Pi Sheng who made movable type out of baked clay as early as A. D. 1049, but the Chinese don't even get mentioned in most American history books.

In fact, the Chinese were doing wood-block printing sometime before A. D. 770. It wasn't done in Europe until 1423.

Anybody who thinks China can be described as

Confucius and kung fu, chopsticks and chow mein knows nothing of a land with the longest continuum of recorded history—3,000 years—in the world. Unfortunately, China's cultural history has been a victim of Western ignorance and residual prejudice.

Just a little over 100 years ago, the British humor magazine, *Punch*, carried this piece of "humorous" verse:

> With their little pig-eyes and their large
> pig-tails,
> And their diet of rats, dogs, slugs, and snails,
> All seems to be game in the frying-pan
> Of that nasty feeder, John Chinaman.
> Sing lie-tea, my sly John Chinaman.
> No fightee, my coward John Chinaman:
> John Bull has a chance—let him, if he can,
> Somewhat open the eyes of John Chinaman.

That libelous bit of doggerel was printed as a send-off for the famed British officer, General Charles Gordon, who was going to lead troops in China. It may have pre-conditioned the general—whose career earned him the name of "Chinese" Gordon—because he later said of the country as a whole, "I do not write about what we saw, as it amounts to nothing. There is nothing of any interest in China; if you have seen one village you have seen all the country."

Hardly. In his enlightening book, British author

Dennis Bloodworth puts some of China's cultural achievements into more accurate historical perspective. He writes: "One thousand years before the birth of Alexander the Great the Chinese were carving jade and weaving silk, casting fine bronze . . . growing wheat, millet and rice . . . painting sophisticated pottery . . . and recording past and prophecy in written language of more than 2,000 characters. In the first millenium before Christ they were making fine armor and using the crossbow that Europe was only to discover in the Middle Ages. . . . They were already working with a calendar of 365½ days to the year."

A Nation of Stereotypes

America was not without its own prejudices. President Theodore Roosevelt had such personal antipathy toward the people and contempt for all things Chinese that the word became a derisive adjective in his vocabulary. He said that if President Woodrow Wilson had his way "Uncle Sam would end up wearing a pigtail"—signifying, to his mind, weakness and cowardliness.

Until Mao came along and shattered the stereotype, most Americans saw China as uncouth, backward and in desperate need of our "enlightened guidance." We saw them as a people who did everything in reverse. They read their books from back to front and up and down. The men had pigtails and the ladies wore trousers. They ate with wooden sticks and loudly belched their approval of a good meal. They stuck needles into their bodies to reduce symptoms of asthma, hypertension and back pain, and took medicine of ground antelope horn mixed with herbs.

Such a strange people. No less a scholar than the nineteenth-century German philosopher, Georg Wilhelm Friedrich Hegel, was persuaded to say, "The history of China has shown no development, so that we cannot concern ourselves with it further."

Which said more about Hegel than it did about China.

But beyond Western ignorance and its own self-serving cultural superiority, the facts still stood. China had discovered physical phenomena and had invented mechanisms that formed the basic ideas on which much future history would rest. Each of us owes a tremendous debt to ancient Chinese perseverance and ingenuity and perhaps the technology for which they now ask us is only fair payment on the debt.

Ancient Needles for Modern Ills

Perhaps the most fascinating export to come from China is that medical phenomenon called acupuncture. It began quite accidentally, Chinese legend says, when it was discovered that arrows shot into one part of a soldier's body could cure illnesses in other parts.

Unbelievable? Yes. True? If not the story, at least

the results are. Aldous Huxley believed it. "That a needle stuck into one's foot should improve the functioning of one's liver is obviously incredible. The only trouble is that, as a matter of . . . fact, it does happen," he wrote in the foreword to a respected book on the subject.

James Reston, noted columnist for *The New York Times*, believes it. General Walter Tkach, Richard Nixon's doctor when he was president, believes it. Prince Bernhard of the Netherlands also believes it. And that is just a fraction of the people who have either personally experienced it or watched it work on others and have validated it as a part of medical science.

Acupuncture dates back to 2600 B.C. and has been used in China ever since then. Only in the past decade, however, has it gained credibility in the West as a respected, reliable means of healing.

The name comes from Latin—*acus*, needle, and *punctura*, puncture. Like all Chinese thought, institutions and practice, it rests on a well-reasoned philosophical base. In this case, the theory behind acupuncture is intimately linked to an ancient Chinese concept called *yin* and *yang*. To the Chinese, this is the most basic formula for the universe. *Yin* is female; *yang* is male. *Yin* is darkness; *yang* is brightness. *Yin* is moon; *yang* is sun. Each is a powerful force in its own right, but is balanced by an equally powerful force. Both are in dynamic opposition, yet together they keep the universe in harmony. They are the energies in the cosmos that continually wax and wane, move in cycles and are always in balance. When one usurps the power of the other, the whole is sacrificed. (Twenty-four hours of sun *or* moon would be an extreme most of us are not prepared to live with.)

The Chinese further believe that man is a small universe in himself. Whatever takes place cosmically also occurs within the confines of the human organism. Since man is a microcosm of this world and its flux, he too will exhibit these vital energy forces. The Chinese call it *ch'i*.

The skilled acupuncturist thinks in this cosmic fashion before he inserts any needles into his patient. His purpose in the treatment is prevention, not cure. If an actual illness should arise, the acupuncturist treats the person, not the illness. Since it is assumed that the problem is an imbalance of *ch'i*, it is important to return a balance to the organism.

This *ch'i* moves through the body along twelve bilateral channels, called meridians. Each meridian has an association with a specific, clearly defined internal organ (i.e., stomach, heart or lungs). On these meridians are some 900 puncture points, each but one-tenth of an inch in diameter and carefully located on detailed charts of the human body.

The acupuncturist inserts stainless steel needles (in the past needles of gold, silver, bone and porcelain were used) into the appropriate puncture point. He varies the depth of the needles and the speed of their insertion. In doing this, the acupuncturist claims he is changing the flow of energy within the body—either stimulating it or sending it off in another direction. The hoped-for result is the restoration of equilibrium to the system and the patient's return to health.

The effectiveness of acupuncture in blocking pain has been carefully documented by Western doctors, many of whom have become believers in the process. Nevertheless, in their demand for an answer that goes beyond the simple *yin* and *yang*, they still want to know *how* it works. Up to now that mystery has eluded them, but there are as many theories as there are doctors.

Chinese practitioners themselves admit they do not really know how or why it works. Dr. Tom Po-chin, an acupuncturist from San Francisco comments, perhaps too simply, "There's nothing miraculous about acupuncture. It's pragmatic medicine, based on thousands of years of application."

Dr. Tkach is emphatic that "acupuncture is not the work of charlatans, nor should it be left to be played with by those who populate the half-world of quackery."

Some argue that acupuncture works because people want it to work. For some that may be true in the same way that a sugar-coated pill prescribed by a doctor "cures" the patient even though there are no physiological benefits at all. Even the American Medical Association admits that if acupunct is nothing more than a placebo, it is certainly one ∪ɪ the most ancient and powerful ones around.

But most doctors have enough humility to accept the benefits even if they don't know how it works. There's precedent for that since medical science still doesn't know how aspirin works, either. Columnist Reston wrote that thirty-six hours after an emergency appendectomy in Peking, he felt severe stomach discomfort. The doctors inserted three needles below Reston's elbow and below the knee. The treatment was combined with what the Chinese called "moxibustion." A doctor burned an herb called *ngai* (wormwood) and held the smoldering material near Reston's abdomen. He said he soon felt better, but offered no speculation about the strange treatment.

There are times when silence is the most appropriate response.

Certainly acupuncture is more than a Chinese hoax. And Western researchers are in no way prepared to write it off as essentially psychological. Although some Chinese practitioners have claimed 90 percent effectiveness, most say acupuncture benefits about 60 to 70 percent of their patients. American doctors suggest that even if the percentage is much smaller than that, these ancient needles will have a growing place in medical treatment for patients with pain which doesn't respond to twentieth-century drugs.

Paper As Well As Books

No Chinese contribution to Western civilization can be more plainly traced than the introduction of paper. (And all the time we thought it was the Egyptians and their papyrus!) Even before its formal invention by Ts'ai Lun precisely dated at A. D. 105, other Chinese scholars were reading books written on narrow, vertical strips of bamboo which, when tied together into a bundle, made one volume. They were bulky and clumsy, but a fifth-century philosopher by the name of Mo Tzu always traveled with three cartloads of such books.

Smaller documents were written on pieces of silk, but this was too expensive for common use. What Ts'ai Lun did was substitute cheaper materials and develop an easy manufacturing process. His name should not be omitted from the list of notable contributors to civilization. Recent discoveries show that as early as A.D. 250 the Chinese were making paper from such things as hemp, the bark of mulberry trees and rags. The Arabic world got the secret in 751 when the Arabs defeated a Chinese army at Samarkand. Among the captives were soldiers who had formerly been paper makers. The new discovery spread throughout the Middle East (displacing papyrus in Egypt in the process) and finally entered Europe through Spain in 1150.

It gradually moved northward, replacing

parchment everywhere—which was a considerable boon to the sheep population. It is doubtful if printing by Gutenberg's movable type would have progressed very rapidly without the introduction of paper, considering that it took the skins of no less than 300 sheep to produce one copy of the Bible on parchment.

While Europe was improving both paper and printing, the Chinese continued to produce their own books and it is estimated that up to the year 1800, more books had been printed in China than in all the rest of the world put together.

They also applied printing to playing cards (these first appeared in Europe in 1377) and to money. Printed paper money came on the Chinese scene during the tenth century and Marco Polo described it in his journal in admiring terms. Europe adopted it later as a matter of convenience, so thank the Chinese the next time you pass a twenty-dollar-bill over the counter. Without their ingenuity you might be rolling twenty pieces of carved stone to the supermarket in a wheelbarrow—also a Chinese invention.

Gunpowder and the Compass

When the Chinese invented gunpowder sometime during the T'ang Dynasty (A.D. 618-906), they very sensibly restricted its use to fireworks. It was not until the later Sung Dynasty (A.D. 1161) that it was turned to purposes of warfare, providing the "bang" for the world's first hand grenades.

The Arabs—them again!—brought the secret of gunpowder westward when they learned about its primary ingredient, saltpeter (they called it "Chinese snow"), from their contacts with China. The first European mention of it is in the thirteenth century by the English philosopher, Roger Bacon, in his *Opus Majus*, an encyclopedia of "useful knowledge."

Perhaps one could debate the blessing of gunpowder, but the compass is less controversial. It also goes further back into antiquity and we are dependent upon the word of Chinese historians as to its first origins.

It was invented, we are told, by the Duke of Chou who lived 1100 years before Christ. He presented to Emperor Cheng Wang five chariots, each outfitted with a "south-pointing needle" to help guide certain foreign ambassadors back to their homelands. It seems to have been subsequently forgotten only to be rediscovered by the astronomer Chang Heng in the second century. The oldest mention of its value to mariners occurs in a work dated in the early twelfth century when it was said to be used by foreign traders—would you believe Arabs!—who regularly sailed from Sumatra to Canton.

The compass isn't mentioned in European literature until a French poet made reference to it about 1190.

Dragons and Earthquakes

The same clever Chang Heng also invented the first seismograph. That occurred about A.D. 132. His device was made of eight copper dragons which were placed on delicate springs around a bowl. In the middle of the bowl was a toad with an open mouth. Each of the dragons held a copper ball in its mouth. When an earthquake occurred, the dragon nearest the location dropped its ball into the mouth of the toad. But a ball dropped one day when no shock was felt and the poor astronomer was ridiculed as a fake—until a messenger arrived telling of an earthquake in a distant province.

But now the Chinese have gone beyond simply measuring earthquakes. Today they are predicting them. The motivation for this new science is high in China, for no other region of the world has suffered such devastating earthquakes. An average of five or six earthquakes with magnitude greater than six have occurred in China each year since 1900.

Although the regime never did release any official estimates of the deaths from the destroyer which struck T'ang-shan in 1976, other sources have put the figure at more than 650,000. It is the second most deadly shaking in recorded history, eclipsed only by another quake which hit China in 1556 after which 820,000 of those killed were recorded by name. The total deaths may have been a million or more.

Even though the T'ang-shan earthquake was not

one of those predicted by Chinese seismologists (the warning signals were said to have been ambiguous) they did score three out of six in that same year. The three tremors were each near magnitude seven on the Richter scale—about one-tenth the intensity of the 1906 San Francisco quake which measured 8.3 in magnitude.

One of the most dramatic successes by the Chinese was their prediction of a serious earthquake in February, 1975. Preliminary indications had led to a warning two months earlier when authorities ordered people out of their homes. The populace lived in tents on the snowy landscape, but finally filtered back to their homes when no tremor materialized. Consequently, it took considerable persuasion to bring about another evacuation, but this time a major quake did occur and thousands of lives are believed to have been saved.

Rather than focus on any single type of warning, the Chinese watch all reported indicators, ranging from unusual animal behavior to changes in pressure-wave velocity. They have reported strange animal behavior before quakes: snakes coming out of their holes, chickens refusing to roost, dogs barking incessantly.

Up to now, the Chinese have remained somewhat aloof from their international colleagues and do not seem interested in applying their experience globally. One writer says, "The world's geophysicists can only eye the tempting possibilities for earthquake research in China and hope that some political upheaval doesn't spoil a chance to study geological ones."

If this should turn out to be an area of international cooperation following China's Great Leap Outward, residents of Los Angeles and San Francisco might one day live—literally—to be grateful.

Where Science Fell Short

The list of early scientific achievements in the Middle Kingdom could go on and on. The Chinese invented the kite and a "sailing carriage" (the first wind-powered car?), porcelain and the iron-chain suspension bridge, watertight compartments and the sternpost rudder. They were the first to use coal and were mining small quantities of it as early as 122 B.C. Chinese astronomers of Confucius' time accurately calculated eclipses and laid out the basis for the Chinese calendar.

In 1064, Chinese astronomers noted the appearance of a supernova, the stellar activity that produced the Crab nebula in Taurus. In that same period they wrote numerous treatises on fruits and flowers, among them possibly the most ancient cataloging of citrus fruits known in any language.

But in spite of these achievements, the Chinese people cannot be called an industrially inventive people. All things scientific had to take their place in the overarching metaphysical world of the *yang* and *yin*. Parmount over physics was the occultism of *feng* shui (wind and water), which refers to the widespread practice of locating homes and graves on sites which were not contrary to the flow of wind and water in the locality.

In other words, to live in harmony with nature was more important than getting caught up in the rat race of so-called progress which left the spirit exhausted.

And all the time we thought it was Thoreau who had discovered that up at Walden's Pond!

The Chinese developed their art forms to a degree of sensitive perfection unsurpassed by any civilization, but until 1912 they were happy with social and economic ways which dated back to the ancients. Even though they had used coal for centuries, they invented nothing to ease the drudgery of mining. One author remarks that the Chinese seemed to have had a "prophetic scorn of labor-saving devices that hectically accelerate the pace of human toil and throw half the population out of work in order to enrich the rest."

It does seem strange that all of these marvelous inventions resulted in no organized technology or body of scientific principles which could be transmitted throughout the social system and from generation to generation.

The answer to the mystery lies in Confucian virtues and Chinese philosophy which the pragmatic Western mind will find hard to comprehend. They simply preferred the quiet and orderly life brought to them by their traditions and learned men over the frantic scramble which results from technological pursuits. The goal of Chinese scholarship was not to bring about man's conquest of nature, but to better understand human society and provide a basis for personal relationships within society.

Who is to say that the goal was invalid? Historian C.P. FitzGerald thinks that it was Sun Yat-sen's unsuccessful drive to streamline the society and modernize China in the early part of the twentieth century which turned the country toward puritanical socialism. He says the Chinese "became disillusioned with the false gods of the West" and "turned restlessly to some other solution."

The Fascinating Face of China

Now once again China is blitzing toward modernization. One can only hope that Teng Hsiao-p'ing remembers his history. As *Time* magazine points out, "Teng's Great Leap Outward can be seen as merely the latest chapter in a 100-year-old struggle between xenophobic conservatives and Westernizing pragmatists."

Even in this book, when we have talked about China, we have implied that there is one thing which is China and one interpretation which can be applied to it. That is much too simplistic a view. As one China-watcher has said, "The most profound thing you can say about China is that it is a big country."

China has many faces and facets. Although most of

its nearly one billion people are of ethnic Chinese stock, there are fifty-four separate national minorities numbering forty million people. These include a handful of Miao and Puyi peasants in the southwestern provinces and 1.7 million Mongols who are the descendants of Genghis Khan. There are the caste-conscious Yi people who have not yet been converted to the idea of a classless society and the 1.3 million Tibetans who live at the top of the world. There are over half-a-million nomads and seven million Chuangs who do not even speak the Chinese language, but that of neighboring Thailand. And the list goes on and on.

Although Mandarin, the dialect of northern China, is the official language, so many other dialects are spoken throughout the country that it is impossible to count them.

This infinite variety of people and languages is spread over a land mass that covers more than one-fifth of the continent of Asia and is 76,400 square miles larger than the United States. China ranks third in size with only Russia and Canada having more territory within their boundaries.

But most of the 3½ million square miles cannot be inhabited. Huge stretches in the three border provinces of Tibet, Sinkiang and Inner Mongolia are either too parched or too frozen for human habitation. These provinces alone make up 40 percent of the country, but contain only 2 percent of the people. In fact, the official tourist handbook says that 95 percent of the population lives in the cities and villages of eastern China.

Thirteen of the world's fifty largest cities are in China. Shanghai, with a population of 12 million, has recently nosed out Tokyo as the most populous city on the planet. Even with this huge urban population, more than 80 percent of the people still live in small villages. With a net gain of 18 million people every year, China will soon pass the one billion mark if, indeed, she hasn't already. Some demographers think that historic billionth birth may have occurred sometime around mid-1978.

This means that China has almost one-fourth of the world's population squeezed into only 7 percent of its land area.

That combination alone creates enormous problems for the nation as it rushes toward the twenty-first century. With that event just two decades away, China finds itself hobbled by the traditions of its past and handicapped by the burden of its current problems.

These loom like two huge mountains which must be removed as China struggles toward the realization of its goal.

The Foolish Old Man

As you might expect, Chinese folklore has a fable which speaks to the problem. Chairman Mao cited it himself, but said the mountains were feudalism and imperialism. I think the story of "The Foolish Old

Man Who Removed the Mountains" also says something to the contemporary situation.

The foolish old man lived long ago in northern China. His house faced south and beyond his doorway stood the two great peaks, Taihang and Wangwu, obstructing the way. With great determination and hoe in hand, the old man decided to move the mountains.

Another greybeard, known as the wise old man, saw the foolish old man and his sons digging and said, "How silly of you to do this! It is quite impossible for you few to dig up these two huge mountains."

The foolish old man replied, "When I die, my sons will carry on; when they die, there will be my grandsons, and then their sons and grandsons, and so on to infinity. High as they are, the mountains cannot grow any higher and with every bit we dig, they will be that much lower. Why can't we clear them away?"

So the old man went on digging, unshaken in his conviction. God was moved by this, and he sent down two angels to carry the mountains away on their backs.

Taking First Steps

The quality of perseverance is deeply embedded in the character of the Chinese people. Whatever else is said about the country, you must say that it has lasted. Considering the number of ancient civilizations over which the dust of centuries blows, just lasting is no mean feat.

Although it has a very long way to go, the ancient land has stirred itself and begun to move. You don't have to agree with the present ideology to pray that the country may have good fortune as it makes the journey. It would seem that a secure and successful China is in the best interest of the whole world. As things get better, the more likely it is that China's new leaders will accelerate the pace for healthy changes.

Within China's soul lies the possibility of greatness. It has achieved it before. There are encouraging signs that it could reach those heights once again.

Now we see only first steps.

But China's ancient sage has a salutary word to say about that. "A journey of a thousand miles," Lao Tzu wrote, "must begin with a single step."

10
China in the Year 2001

This is not the end. It is not even the beginning of the end. But it is, perhaps, the end of the beginning.

Sir Winston Churchill

In a delicious bit of lofty rhetoric, the late U.S. Senator Kenneth Wherry once remarked: "With God's help we'll lift Shanghai up and up, ever up, until it's just like Kansas City."

Kansas City?

Even admitting—as the song tells us—that "everything's up-to-date in Kansas City" the Nebraska senator's dream scarcely seems like either a desirable or realizable goal.

And besides, if the musical is to be believed, Kansas City had "gone about as far as they can go."

Not so China.

After over 3,000 years of recorded history, it still has only just begun. The propaganda images portray the country as one huge industrial complex broken up by lush, productive agricultural communes. The reality is something else again and to see it you have only to step off the tourist track and wander down small urban streets or through tiny rural villages.

In truth, China is still desperately poor. If the areas seen by tourists are typical of the whole country, then the best that can be said is that the people are (1) adequately, but minimally, fed; (2) in reasonably good health; and (3) sufficiently, if unstylishly, clothed. Beyond that it is difficult to see any real improvement in the standard of living.

One worker admits candidly, "We are very backward," but adds, "If you return in ten years, you will find everything changed. We are going to make it all over again, all new and modern in ten years' time."

The goal and commitment are commendable; the time frame is without doubt too optimistic. Certainly not in ten years and probably not in twenty years.

But even if everything isn't "all new and modern," what will China be like in the year 2001? Speculating is a fascinating exercise. It is also risky, especially when you are speculating about China. The country has this strange way of making 90-degree and even 180-degree turns without much advance signaling.

Take the current situation. De-Maoification is occurring at a dizzying pace. Who would have guessed it two years before? The people are being softened up to accept doctrines so contrary to classical Marxism that even to mention them before the death of Mao would have brought prison and probably death. One marvels at the ability of a whole nation to do an instant about-face in its views of a leader who for thirty years was portrayed as a demigod. Now when talking about the discredited Gang of Four—all Mao cohorts, including his wife—some Chinese will hold up five fingers, identifying Mao himself with these villains who are blamed for all the ills of the past decade.

Such ideological flexibility has long been required for survival in China and it seems to have been bred into the character of the people. The same crowds who used to shout in Tienanmen Square, "Long live Chairman Mao! A long, long life to him!" are today putting up wall posters which accuse the "great helmsman" of being "fascist" and "dictatorial."

So understanding that unforeseen events could bring about more turns of 90 degrees or 180 degrees, let us speculate about China in the twenty-first century.

More Freedom Likely

China has never known democracy as the West understands the term, not even under the beloved Sun Yat-sen who founded the first republic. Certainly his successor, Generalissimo Chiang Kai-shek, was something less than the great democrat his defenders made him out to be. Authoritarian rulers have been the norm of China.

Perhaps nothing more by way of democracy was possible for a people so numerous, so diverse and so illiterate. Most Americans have a strange way of viewing the world through rose-colored glasses ground to match our idealism. This unrealistic view of the world then causes us to believe that every country can—and should—have our form of government. Actually, a rather large degree of social and educational sophistication is required to successfully bring off a government "of the people, by the people and for the people."

China had neither of these, as is also true of many newly-independent countries in the developing world. We would do well to try to understand their peculiar situations instead of willy-nilly trying to make them all over to look like Kansas City.

When thinking about "freedom" in the new China, it is also important to know that the country has never prized individualism as much as we have in the West. It is simply not woven into the fabric of Chinese life. The family, the clan, the community all take precedence over one's individual desires, and to do something simply because it "makes me feel good" is considered the ultimate in selfishness.

Consequently, freedom also must be understood as relative. However, a people who have scarcely been allowed private thoughts for thirty years are suddenly feeling the exhilaration of being able to exercise their voices.

Bannered the Peking *People's Daily:* "Let the

people say what they wish. The heavens will not fall
. . . a range of opinions is good for a revolutionary
party. When people are free to speak, it means the
party and the government have strength and
confidence."

Westerners would have seen that as a call for
unrestrained free speech. No Chinese read it that
way. He knows where the subtle boundaries are that
restrict him to the areas of propriety and
responsibility. He also knows where the *Pao-wei*
(secret police) are, and he knows that this machinery
for party discipline hums with a well-oiled efficiency
to crush those who push the boundaries too far.

Nonetheless, the posters started going up on
Peking's "democracy wall" and crowds gathered to
read and ask questions of foreigners. They wanted to
talk about other political systems, especially the
one in the United States. One of the wall posters was
addressed to President Jimmy Carter and was
signed by "The Human Rights Group." It called on
the president to "pay attention to the state of human
rights in China. We do not want to repeat the tragic
life of the Soviet people in the Gulag Archipelago."

That particular poster didn't stay up long and the
message relayed by the regime in having it removed
would not be lost on those who put it up or on others
who might get carried away in a burst of enthusiasm.

However, the *People's Daily* had already
complained that "the legal rights and interests of
citizens are badly infringed." As proof, the paper

cited the closing of rural markets, reduction of rations and confiscation of private property. It urged the adoption of new civil and criminal codes to guard the rights of the people. In the wake of that series of articles published in Peking, twenty-nine pages were posted in Shanghai, quoting at length from the American Declaration of Independence. The writers concluded that "if the government abuses people's rights, the people have the right to abolish the government and create a new one."

That might seen tame anywhere else, but in China it is heady stuff.

Only a major reversal of political policy would send China back to the silent pre-Teng days. If Teng can hold on to his power and if he can put his own hand-picked successor in place, China in the twenty-first century will be speaking and discussing many crucial subjects with the rest of the world, and each side will be learning from the other.

That would be a plus for all mankind.

But don't look for any kind of "free speech" movement such as that which swept the campus of the University of California at Berkeley in the 1960s.

Even in twenty-first century China, there will still be propriety and responsibility.

China and the Soviet Union

Could those Russian officers I talked to in Leipzig way back in 1966 possibly have been right? Might there sometime be an alliance between Russia and the United States to fight a common enemy, the traditionally feared "yellow peril"? What are relationships between China and the Soviet Union apt to look like twenty years from now?

It will help us speculate regarding the future if we know something about the past.

From the first contact between the two powers in 1619, Russia and China have traveled a rocky road. It took seventy years for the Russians to get trading rights from the Chinese because the Czar's envoys refused to *kowtow* before the emperor. Finally, when the symbolic submission was made in 1689, the ambassador went back to Moscow bearing the Treaty of Nerchinsk.

Because of their common Marxist ideology, the two countries became cozy in the period between 1920 and 1960. Russia had won the support of the educated Chinese when, as early as 1918, the Czarist government unilaterally renounced all special privileges it had been enjoying along with the Western nations as a result of the "unequal treaties." Thus at the very moment China was struggling to extricate herself from the tyranny of the warlords and the bondage of feudalism, Russia was treating the nation as an equal and not as a semi-colony.

This attitude gained points for Russia, and there was much admiration for the Communist rulers even by Sun Yat-sen, father of the Chinese republic. His successor, Chiang Kai-shek, sent his son—now the

President of the Republic of China on Taiwan—to Russia for twelve years. Both Mao Tse-tung and the Generalissimo had their early infatuation with Russia. Mao's lasted longer than Chiang's, but it too was over by 1963.

The embrace of the Russian bear turned into nothing more than an unloving squeeze and China wanted out. However, as the Papa Bear of the whole international Communist movement, Russia wanted all the disciples of Marx to pay homage at the bear's den called the Kremlin. It was, they signaled, China's turn to *kowtow*.

But Mao was as proud as any emperor and the resulting differences became a full-fledged split in 1963. Since then, relations between the two Communist powers have been as frosty as a Siberian morning.

As late as 1978, Russia made an overture to patch up the quarrel: "The existing state of affairs leads to the creation of an atmosphere of mutual distrust, to the heightening of tensions in inter-state relations," the Soviets wrote.

The Chinese testily replied that they would not be satisfied with "hollow statements" and suggested "if the Soviet side desires to improve Sino-Soviet relations, it should take concrete actions that solve practical problems." Among the "concrete actions" the Chinese wanted was a withdrawal of Russian troops from Mongolia and the border areas with China, a plege to honor the existing border on a temporary basis and an immediate conference to permanently resolve the border dispute.

Moscow fired a salvo charging that "hostility to the Soviet Union continues to be elevated to the rank of state policy in China" and China shot back that the Russians were staging a "propaganda stunt."

The 4,500-mile border will continue to be a military flashpoint because the rivers which comprise some of the boundary will still thaw in the spring, giving the two giants reason to keep on arguing lines of demarcation. Although Russia enjoys playing war games within sight of the Chinese divisions stationed on the border, an outright military action seems increasingly unlikely.

The reason is that by 2001, China will have a nuclear arsenal more than adequate to hold her own with the Soviet Union. Except for that nuclear capability which China now possesses, most of the military hardware acquired by China over the next twenty years will probably come from the U.S.A., augmented by some purchases from France and Great Britain. This will give the Western powers considerable interest in what happens, and their "presence-by-proxy" could add stability to the region.

There is one caveat. The possibility of a preemptive strike by Russia against China's western provinces cannot be entirely ruled out. However, this will become less likely with the passing of time and China's growing strength.

Rather than a direct border confrontation, it is more reasonable to expect the two powers to struggle with each other through secondary conflicts, e.g., Vietnam and Cambodia. Russia seems determined to establish a strong Asian presence and China is greatly exercised over what she calls "hegemony."

Forecast: Squally, with considerable lightning and thunder while the storm continues to hang on the horizon.

Relations with the U.S.A.

The lightning speed with which China decided to normalize relations with the United States indicates the urgent need which Teng Hsiao-p'ing felt for things the Western power can provide. A part of that urgency may well have been linked with the Russian problem. It certainly did not arise out of friendship.

What will China gain? Primarily, access to technology and expertise. Progress in the two areas of agriculture and science are at the top of Teng's goals. He simply went to the place where help was most readily available. Secondarily, consumer goods. Life in China is still spartan and there is no way the country can gear up to meet the consumer demand which will grow as the nation emerges from its stifling recent past. Once again, it was a matter of going where the goods were most readily available.

Certainly, military hardware is going to be high on China's shopping list. Her army is poorly equipped and the generals must make up in numbers what it lacks in weapons sophistication. Purchases in this area are not expected to be large at first, however, because of a shortage of capital and the higher priority placed on the other modernizations.

It could also be argued that China has strengthened her position with Russia simply by stepping out of isolation and establishing a link with Russia's major contender in the world. In the field of diplomacy one frequently sees the application of an old principle: "The enemy of thine enemy is a friend."

But normalization is not just a one-way street. The United States also stands to benefit from this mutual recognition. It must be admitted that our primary motive was not friendship either. Probably the biggest advantage is in the area of trade. With an increasingly disastrous balance of payments problem, the U.S. badly needed new trading partners. It must have seemed like a dream come true to have nearly one-fourth of the world open up as a marketplace with just one stroke of a pen.

Think what that means. Pharmaceutical executives get ecstatic over the prospect of selling just one aspirin tablet each to one billion Chinese! To say nothing of Big Macs, Coca-Cola, Instamatics and Chevettes.

The prospect of trade is only one advantage. The gains in the political field are as great in their way as commercial opportunities are to the U.S. economy. As long as China remained aggressive and unfriendly, the U.S. found its options quite limited in negotiations with the Russians. Through recognition of China the president has added an important card to his hand which opens up numerous new negotiating options and keeps Russia nervous at the same time.

In addition, an open and outgoing China is less dangerous to the world than one which is plotting behind its borders. Now that it has joined the community of nations, China has a forum with the rest of the world for dialogue, debate and compromise. History shows that, speaking generally, China has never been expansionistic. Mostly she lost more than she ever took. The exception to that is Tibet where China seemed to be: (1) trying to secure her borders with India and (2) reclaiming territory she felt was hers by historical right. That may not have been adequate justification for the brutal action, but you don't have to agree with the reasons in order to understand them from the Chinese perspective.

The confrontation with the United States in Korea was not an attempt to annex territory. China saw the Communist government of North Korea threatened and moved to preserve it. China has been the hand manipulating the fingers in Cambodia and of the revolutionary movements in Thailand and Burma. This is simply evidence that the Chinese Communists have not given up their goal of fomenting revolution, but that is not the same as conquering countries for annexation. Certainly China has not been as hungry for territory as the Russian bear.

A Mixed Blessing

For good or bad, normalization of relations with China stands to be considered as the single most important diplomatic move made by the United States in the last half of the twentieth century.

That does not mean it won't be a mixed blessing. We dare not forget that the regime is still Marxist and has never renounced the Marxist goal of revolution. Teng is not that much different from Mao. The vice premier said in 1974: "Countries want independence, nations want liberation and the people want revolution—this is the irresistible trend of history."

Peking's influence will be pervasive from now on. There will be a new China lobby in this country which will press us to support Chinese Communist goals. They will get support for their campaigns from some of the media, students and political liberals. The public needs to be awake, alert and discerning. The lobby will push Congress for concessions on trade tariffs, goods quotas and other favorable commercial considerations for China. Pro-Peking organizations can certainly be counted on to exert pressure through the media for the Congress and the president to cut off military aid to Taiwan.

None of this should come as a surprise. It is a

matter of record that the Chinese know what they want and how to go about getting it. Mao spoke the strategy in 1945: "How to give 'tit for tat' depends on the situation. Sometimes not going to negotiations is tit for tat; sometimes, going to negotiations is tit for tat." There is no reason for alarm, but abundant reason for vigilance.

For 2001, the prospects look encouraging if both sides remain strong. A strong China is in our own best interest. The basis for the continuing relationship must be that of mutual advantage, not sentimental friendship. That doesn't mean we shouldn't cultivate personal relationships with Chinese people. Obviously we should and certainly they are capable of responding. One of the recent posters in Peking declared: "I want to speak English with American people." But personal friendships and national interests are not synonymous. And lying deep in the Chinese character is an innate suspicion and prejudice against foreign things and people. Considering the way foreigners have treated China through the centuries, they may feel this attitude is not ill-founded.

A Chinese philosopher once wrote: "Throughout the ages, the Chinese have had only two ways of looking at foreigners: up to them as superior beings or down on them as wild animals. They have never been able to treat them as friends, as people like themselves."

Twenty years are not going to change the Chinese

character which has been forming over centuries. If we understand that and do not expect more from each other than we are able to give, there is no reason why mutual respect and mutual interests—if not friendship—cannot provide a basis for the two countries to live in peace.

Taiwan: The Big Question

The biggest furor in the United States over the recognition of the People's Republic of China was the severing of diplomatic ties with the Republic of China, or Taiwan. This, too, has an interesting history which must be explored in order to understand the present and look into the future.

The decision to establish diplomatic relations with Peking also resolved an ancillary, but equally important, question: Who rules China? For nearly thirty years we have perpetuated the fiction that the government on Taiwan ruled China. It is important to differentiate between the *de facto* rulers and those who claimed to be the legal government. Chiang Kai-shek insisted that he was head of the only legal government, and the U.S.A.—pushed by the old China lobby—did not disagree. What happened was that with the Communist victory in 1949, the Generalissimo fled the mainland to Taiwan with between one million and two million officers and soldiers, civil servants, Kuomintang Party members and the families of them all.

Since Taiwan was a part of the Republic of

China—so declared by the Allies after World War II—Chiang proclaimed the island as seat of his government for all China and announced his intention to return and liberate the mainland. Even though Chiang is dead and his son governs in his place, the goal of liberating the mainland is still a cornerstone of the Taiwan government's policy. However, there is no reasonable possibility that it can ever happen.

President Carter's decision to recognize the mainland government simply acknowledged the realities. After thirty years, the question of legal or illegal is purely academic. However, many critics feel that the president may have given away too much on the Taiwan issue.

But before that question can be decided, there is a more basic one: To whom does Taiwan belong? Is the Nationalist claim valid? This is where we need to look at history.

Although their ancestors migrated from China between the fifteenth and sixteenth centuries, the Taiwanese people have developed their own language and culture apart from that of mainland China. For nearly 400 years, however, Taiwan has been someone else's colony. First, it was the Dutch who came in 1624. They followed by the Portuguese who named the island Formosa, meaning "beautiful." Then came the Chinese during the Ming Dynasty, who were replaced by the Japanese in 1895. After an occupation of fifty years, the

Japanese were beaten in World War II—although Taiwan was not the battleground—and gave way to Chiang Kai-shek and the Nationalists.

From the Taiwanese viewpoint, it was simply one dominant power being substituted for another—none of whom were chosen by the Taiwanese themselves. For those who believe that Taiwan is the last bastion of Chinese democracy and should be maintained under its present government for that reason, it bears pointing out that the fifteen million native Taiwanese have lived under martial law ever since the Nationalists arrived.

They have been denied fundamental political and human rights. For example, although the native population constitutes 85 percent of the island's people, they were given only 5 percent of the seats in the national assembly. This is the nation's parliament which meets only once every six years to elect the president. In the national legislature, which passes laws regulating the affairs of all citizens, native Taiwanese get only 10 percent of the vote. The Kuomintang justifies this disparity on the basis that they represent the much larger mainland population and, therefore, deserve a larger share of electoral and legislative power.

With large financial grants from the U.S. government and under protection of the U.S. Seventh Fleet, Taiwan has become one of the economic miracles of the world. Per capita income has risen from $280 in 1968 to $1,400 in 1978, more than three times that of China. Agricultural production per acre is one of the highest in the world. A land reform program, launched in the 1950s, did away with absentee landlords and has virtually eliminated rural destitution.

Along with business and agriculture, Christianity also prospered. Religious liberty was fostered by the late Generalissimo and Madame Chiang Kai-shek, both practicing Christians. A large force of missionaries, many of whom were formerly on the mainland, are resident in Taiwan. It will be difficult for them and their sending agencies to be objective regarding the government of the country which has shown such a benign attitude toward Christian evangelization. Official friendliness to Christianity covers a multitude of other governmental sins—and this remains one of the principal dilemmas for Christian missions in numbers of countries, of which Taiwan is by no means the most dramatic example.

The other side of the coin is that there is a continuing underground current calling for the independence of Taiwan. It is growing and is supported by more than a few church leaders—especially in the Presbyterian church which is predominant among native Taiwanese. The government regards the movement as treasonous and crushes it anytime it begins to surface.

Both by area and population—17 million—Taiwan qualifies to be an independent nation. Given the present and foreseeable emotions between Taiwan and the mainland, however, even if independence could be achieved apart from the Kuomintang—an unlikely event—the result would almost certainly be a continuing state of siege between the island and the mainland.

Thus missions face an agonizing dilemma. How do they remain loyal to and supportive of Taiwanese Christians without committing themselves to the attitudes and practices of the present government or—conversely—to its overthrow?

One great concern is that non-Christians in Taiwan's government may use President Carter's "sell-out" of their country as an argument that Christians cannot be trusted and that the church's liberty to evangelize should be curtailed.

Exploring the Options

If speculating about China proper in the twenty-first century is like looking through a glass darkly, then trying to see the future of Taiwan can be compared to peering out into midnight.

Let's explore some of the options available, providing the Communist regime on the mainland doesn't seek its own "liberation" of Taiwan by force. Teng Hsiao-p'ing says he has "taken note" of President Carter's wish that reunification should take place peacefully, but the vice premier added, "We cannot tie our hands on this matter."

One option, but one which almost certainly would be rejected by the present government of Taiwan, is to exchange its goal of "liberation" of the mainland for autonomy. It seems impossible for Nationalists to agree to this solution, however. It is that goal of returning victoriously to the mainland—which many fervently believe is possible—that has given Taiwan unity. Without that goal and the strong military force which supports it, the indigenous Taiwanese might mount a claim to their rightful place. The resulting turmoil would undoubtedly bring swift intervention from the mainland.

The option which Teng seems to be pursuing is to woo Taiwan with soft words. He has offered negotiations and a place in the government to President Chiang Ching-kuo of Taiwan. It is doubtful that Teng is in a hurry. Time—and the healing that comes with it—certainly favors him. This is especially true if the government on the mainland becomes more open and humane.

Peking has already begun its campaign to encourage the Chinese on Taiwan to come home. Mainlanders are being softened up to welcome these former "U.S. imperialist lackeys." It must have been quite a shock to Peking television viewers when in late 1978 a documentary on Taiwan was shown which didn't jibe with previous propaganda portraying the island as a cesspool of oppression and poverty. Taipei was depicted as the prosperous city it is, well-run private farms were shown approvingly and Buddhist monks were filmed at worship.

Don't be put off by the shrill rhetoric from Taipei

which says, "Never!" Reunification could happen. Don't forget it is Chinese, not alien, blood that flows through the veins on both sides of the East China Sea. Given time and another generation, it could just happen.

Confucius once said, "When you have faults, do not fear to abandon them." In Asia, the problem is that admitting fault also causes you to lose face. If a face-saving way can be found so that nobody is forced to "come back," but both simply get together, pragmatism might win out over face.

Say in the twenty-first century.

In the meantime, Taiwan has another option. This one is called "playing the Russian card." It was proposed at an emergency meeting of the Nationalists' Central Committee after Washington and Peking announced they would exchange ambassadors—and was flatly rejected. Nonetheless, it is certainly an option, if for no reason other than to shake up Washington.

Parris Chang, professor of political science at Pennsylvania State University, comments that "The Nationalists have a history of working with Moscow when their requests for Western support have been spurned, and many Nationalist leaders have close ties with the Soviets."

Perhaps some of those strongest ties are with Taiwan's president, who is Chiang Kai-shek's eldest son. It was he whom Chiang sent to Russia when he was a young man. Chiang Ching-kuo lived and worked there for twelve years. He married a Russian wife. The Soviet Union certainly has his ear if they want to send him a message—and they just might make him an offer he would find hard to refuse.

If Taiwan chooses not to play the Russian card, it will be in spite of Soviet coaxing. A move towards Russia would undoubtedly please the Soviet leaders because it would embarrass both Washington and Peking. However, because of very lucrative trade agreements with the United States ($7.5 billion in 1978), it would be risky for Taipei.

The best guess is that Taiwan will resist this option of moving into the Soviet orbit unless there is a direct and serious military threat from the mainland. Then they just might view a protected spot as a satellite in the Soviet orbit as the lesser of two evils.

Through a Glass Darkly

Whatever China looks like on the outside when the twenty-first century rolls around, the cultural landscape inside China is not apt to be radically different from today. The reason is that twenty years in the history of a people is not very long—especially if those people have a 3,000-year tradition which has produced minimal social progress.

Yet for the first time in her 3,000 years, China does seem to be in a hurry. Teng gives the impression that he isn't prepared to sit by and allow the *yang* and the *yin* to move unaided in the natural order. He is ready to force change.

Here is what China in the twenty-first century may look like—but, remember, we are looking through a glass darkly.

(1) Chinese Communism in the twenty-first century will be less revolutionary than the original variety. This might make Mao turn over in his grave, but Teng is already moving to correct the excesses of the Cultural Revolution. Persons considered "bourgeois" during that three-year madness are being rehabilitated. At a rubber factory in Canton, "six former bourgeois owners" have been brought back to work in administrative and production jobs.

The vice premier is sending the message through the ranks that the new China wants a person's technical knowledge, not his political purity. He indicated long ago that he favors at least some private ownership of land. Even during Mao's lifetime, Teng asserted that "private farming is all right as long as it raises production, just as it doesn't matter whether a cat is black or white as long as it catches mice." He was later condemned as an "unrepentant capitalist roader" for that bit of Marxist heresy, but he managed to survive.

"Expert" will still be better than "red."

(2) Increasing cultural and student exchanges between China and the outside world—particularly the United States—will encourage the Chinese people to pursue an even more capitalistic life style. As a race, the Chinese know how to enjoy good

things and it has been a long time since they have had a chance to indulge their fancies. A bicycle will no longer be seen as the ultimate status symbol. The ownership of private cars will increase substantially.

(3) Tourism will be one of the biggest money earners for the country. In 1978, about 700,000 foreigners—80 percent of them Chinese from Hong Kong and Macao—visited China. That was nearly double the number in 1977. The availability of facilities will be about the only restriction on the tourist traffic in the future.

However, China has already contracted for the construction and operation of first-class tourist facilities and these in themselves will stimulate the Chinese taste for consumer goods and luxury items.

After signing a $500 million deal for a chain of luxury hotels across the country, Paul Sheeline, chairman of Intercontinental Hotels, said, "The Chinese want to go first class. They told us to build the kind of hotel where the president of the Bank of Tokyo could comfortably hold a reception for several hundred people."

(4) With the help of American technology, extensive development of its oil deposits will give China the economic leverage it must have to buy the raw materials and consumer goods it will need as it enters the twenty-first century. All during Mao's reign, the Communist Party boasted that China was beholden to no one. They had no debts, no friends to be paid off, no mortgage on their future.

Now all that is changing. Foreign debts are mounting. The *Far Eastern Economic Review* reports that "Major U.S. banks are preparing to loan billions of dollars to China . . . and are waiting only for Peking to give the go-ahead."

By 2001, China will have accounts payable all over the world. This alone will lock the nation so tightly into the Western economic orbit that retreat will be exceptionally difficult, if not almost impossible.

(5) China has been a nuclear power since 1964. By the year 2001, she will be a major nuclear force in the region and in the world. If the national economy doesn't falter, she will have the economic capacity to rival American and Soviet stockpiles and delivery systems. That, coupled with population, influence, increased wealth, human dynamism and world-wide acceptance will give China the status Mao was struggling to gain.

Ironically, it will not have been Mao's thought that made the difference. It will have been what he damned as being antithetical to the Chinese revolution—nothing more or less than "decadent" American capitalism.

(6) With increasing personal freedom to dissent, ancient philosophical and religious beliefs will have a chance to reemerge. Even in the new technocracy, there will be some "free spirits" in China who may desire once again to espouse classical Taoism—a philosophy that says, "Let nature take its course . . . don't struggle . . . just let things be."

As with the United States in the 1960s, some will certainly turn their backs on political authority like a third-century Chinese "hippie" who left this Taoist inscription:

As the sun rises I get up,
As the sun sets I go to rest.
I dig a well for my drink,
I till the fields for my food.
What has the power of the emperor to do with me?

(7) While older religions will undoubtedly emerge again—every major Chinese philosophy/religion has gone through its death throes later to be revived—so, too, will there be a new expression of the Christian faith. It will come out of the church which has already been underground for thirty years.

Its form will not be familiar to the West, for it will be noninstitutional. It will be based on relationships in the body of Christ, not on formal structure. It will not bear Western denominational labels which have always been foreign to China.

It will be a church of incredible purity, for it will have come through the fires of suffering. It will be a church stripped down by persecution to only the essential matters of faith; there has been no room for excess cultural baggage. The people who are part of it will have no time for Western theological and ecclesiastical frivolities.

They will be passionately in love with the simple, uncluttered Word of God for it is this that has sustained them. They are likely to have little patience with a civil Christianity which substitutes a cultural veneer for a deep experience with Jesus Christ.

In the twenty-first century, some of these believers will be coming to the United States and other Western countries. They will likely be shocked and disturbed by what they see of so-called Christian nations. They may deliver the kind of jeremiads which have come from another prophet, Alexandr Solzhenitysn. If so, we probably won't like them because they aren't upbeat enough for a church that is "rich, and increased with goods, and has need of nothing."

But in truth, they will be the very ones we ought to listen to, for they will be God's missioners to us.

In the year 2001.

And one of them may be moved to say, "With God's help we'll lift Kansas City up and up, ever up, until it's just like Shanghai."

For free information on how to receive
the international magazine

LOGOS JOURNAL

also Book Catalog

Write: Information -

LOGOS JOURNAL CATALOG
Box 191
Plainfield, NJ 07061